Crisis Management

Responding from the Heart

NASPA
Student Affairs Administrators
in Higher Education

Crisis Management

Responding from the Heart

Kristin S. Harper, Brent G. Paterson and Eugene L. Zdziarski II
Editors

NASPA
Student Affairs Administrators
in Higher Education

Crisis Management: Responding from the Heart
Copyright © 2006 by the National Association of Student Personnel Administrators (NASPA), Inc. Printed and bound in the United States of America. All rights reserved. No part of this book may be reproduced in any form or by any electronic or mechanical means without written permission from the publisher. First edition.

Additional copies may be purchased by contacting the NASPA publications department at 301-638-1749 or visiting http://www.naspa.org/publications.

ISBN 0-931654-39-4

Contents

Preface

Kristin S. Harper

Sometimes the unique skills of individuals come together to create something that none of the group could have created on their own. Response to a campus crisis requires this type of coordinated effort. Once such an effort is running smoothly, a shared language develops to describe aspects of the work, in which the meanings of words are tied to the common experience of the group. Thus, when a group of colleagues who have developed an effective critical incident response team try to explain how to replicate that team at other institutions, they may have difficulty finding the right words.

When we first started discussing a publication on crisis response in student affairs, the concept of "doing the right thing" emerged as a theme. However, the "right thing" is likely to vary with the situation and the person. Knowing the right thing to do depends on personal character, possession of a moral compass that points in the right direction. Can you train someone to know what the right thing is?

Once the members of your group are satisfied that they share a mutual understanding of the meaning of doing the right thing, they can trust each other and support each other's decisions. This trust may not be based on the person's professional skills and qualifications or years of experience but rather on his or her understanding of what constitutes doing the right thing. Current literature offers training in critical incident response procedures. The literature gives us a firm foundation on which to develop the processes necessary for an effective institutional response to crisis. The editors and authors of this book delve a bit further by asking what is at the heart of this kind of work—what makes responding to crisis an extraordinary experience, and how do we identify the people who do this work well and help them stay healthy?

Which comes first, the chicken or the egg? That is, do people who do well in crisis response (those who have the skills to respond with head and heart) learn these skills or are they just "that kind of people?" If we believe that the response is a learned behavior, how do we teach someone to know the right thing to do for each situation? Once we identify those who have the ability to know the right thing to do, how do we supervise them in a way that encourages this ability without allowing it to become a burden or emotionally debilitating? And how does one maintain a personal life and still do this all-encompassing kind of work?

In the discussions that led to the development of this book, the editors decided that the best way to approach these questions would be to identify people who have experience doing the right thing and ask them to share their experience. All the elements of effective response to crisis can't be learned from a book, but the ideas shared in this publication can generate discussion and provide some insight into how others have put together responses that involved heart and head. While other publications and manuals focus on crisis response plans, this book gives examples of how people did the right thing, how they felt about doing it, and how they cared for themselves or sought the assistance of others to continue to do good work.

This publication provides examples of good practice grouped by incident and by persons involved in crisis response, from the parents of a student to a senior student affairs officer. The authors share how they worked through a crisis intellectually, emotionally, and spiritually, and how their work affected the lives of people involved in the crisis as well as their own family members.

As our world has become more vulnerable, campuses have put time and money into preparing for the unexpected and developing effective procedures to respond to crises. This publication acknowledges the other dimension of crisis response and gives *feelings* the same level of importance as *procedures*. Doubt and uncertainty can be debilitating to the process, while the strength that comes from doing the right thing can energize the process and contribute to a positive outcome. All the emotions involved in crisis response can take a toll on campus responders and, without appropriate supervision, can lead to difficulties at work and at home.

This book is not the last word in developing effective crisis response; rather, we hope readers will be encouraged to discuss their own experiences in doing the right thing. We also hope that these discussions—on moral and ethical issues, and on the work's emotional toll and its impact on home and family—will result in better professional preparation programs for these workers. And finally, for those who supervise crisis responders, we look for understanding and clarification of the importance of this work and support for all facets of the crisis response process, from initial response to debriefing and personal support.

As we worked on this publication, Hurricanes Katrina and Rita hit the Gulf Coast, and our country faced the worst natural disaster in centuries. Colleges across the Gulf Coast of Louisiana, Mississippi, and Texas were forced to evacuate students and close their heavily damaged campuses for the entire fall semester. In some cases, institutions had a crisis response plan; in other cases, they responded to the circumstances as well as they could. Across the country, other colleges and universities opened their doors to the displaced students, allowing them admission and registration without reference to transcript, course placement, or enrollment caps. We want to recognize our colleagues at the colleges and universities directly affected by the hurricanes as well as those who responded to the needs of evacuees and displaced students. The concern of these people and their institutions made a difference in the lives of college students and others.

With these natural disasters so fresh in our memories, we should be more committed than ever to reviewing our campus and student affairs crisis plans and ensuring that we are able to do the right thing.

Chapter 1

Crisis in the Context of Higher Education

Eugene L. Zdziarski II

Administrators in higher education face many demands on their time and resources. Often, the time for crisis management planning or consideration of proactive and preventive measures is severely limited. With the multitude of other priorities vying for our attention, it is easy to get complacent; we may be lulled into thinking that it won't happen to us, not on our campus. But history shows that crises strike campuses large and small, urban and rural.

On August 1, 1966, on the campus of one of the largest universities in the country, the world watched a crisis unfold on television. Charles Whitman, a former U.S. Marine, climbed to the top of the Texas Tower on the University of Texas campus after killing his wife and mother. With an arsenal of weapons, he killed 14 people and injured dozens of others (Rollo, 1999). Television news live coverage and on-scene reporting were in their infancy. The vivid pictures of this incident provided people across the country with the reality that our campuses were not immune from crisis.

In May 1970, at the height of the protests against the Vietnam War, National Guard troops were sent onto the Kent State University campus to disperse a large group of protestors. Protestors threw rocks at the troops, who were armed with live ammunition. At first teargas was fired into the crowd, but then shots were fired, killing four students and wounding nine (Rollo, 1999; May 4 Task Force, 1996). This incident sparked a huge reaction across the country. Antiwar efforts expanded and demonstrations erupted on campuses throughout the nation, causing classes to be cancelled and campuses to shut down for periods of time.

In 1986, a 19-year-old freshman, Jeanne Ann Cleary, was raped and murdered in her residence hall room at Lehigh University. It was later learned that her assailant had entered the residence hall through a series of doors that were either propped open or unlocked (Cleary & Cleary, 2001).

In 1998, the death of a student again fueled a passionate response from institutions around the country. In a rural area outside of Laramie, Wyoming, the body of Matthew Sheppard, a University of Wyoming student, was discovered tied to a fence. Matthew, an openly gay young man, had been brutally beaten by two men because of his sexual orientation (Hurst, 1999).

None of us will ever forget the impact of September 11. While the attacks themselves did not occur on college campuses, the collapse of the Twin Towers had major consequences for institutions in the New York City and Washington, D.C., areas, and sent a wave of fear throughout the rest of the country that caused many campuses to close. The events of that day will have a lasting impact on how Americans live and how university administrators approach potential campus crises.

The impact of Hurricane Katrina and the devastation it wrought on Louisiana, Mississippi, and Alabama will surely have a lasting impact on the way we plan for hurricanes and floods. Institutions around the country opened their doors to students displaced by the hurricane, offering them late admission and in-state tuition. Students organized efforts to raise money, to collect food and supplies, and to volunteer in the recovery effort.

History has shown that crises can and do strike our campuses, and we have a responsibility to plan for and be prepared to respond to them. However, our plans and preparations should not be limited to catastrophic events. Crises come in all shapes and sizes, and we need to be prepared for all of them.

What Is a Crisis?

What is a crisis? How should we define the term? While there is general agreement and understanding of the concept, there is no common or established theoretical construct (Auerbach & Kilmann, 1977; Hermann, 1972), and a standard or widely accepted definition does not exist (Coombs, 1999; Hermann, 1972; Levitt, 1997). Part of the reason for the lack of a common definition of crisis is the number of different disciplines that use the term and contribute to the literature (Hermann, 1963). Crisis management spans a variety of disciplines, including business, education, public administration, communications, political science, and psychology. These disciplines define crisis and address crisis management from different perspectives, causing what one author refers to as a "fragmentation" of the literature (Coombs, 1999). But the literature does provide a number of common characteristics associated with a crisis: negative event or outcome, threat to people and property, surprise or sudden event, and disruption to operations.

Most of the literature portrays crisis as a negative event or outcome that poses a threat to the organization (e.g., Abent, 1999; Albrecht, 1996; Dressel, 1981; Hermann, 1963, 1972; Holsti, 1978; Koovor-Misra, 1995; Lerbinger, 1997; Pauchant & Mitroff, 1992; Phelps, 1986). Specifically, crises can threaten an organization's mission and goals (Hermann, 1963, 1972; Holsti, 1978; Koovor-Misra, 1995); its profitability (Levitt, 1997); its reputation (Abent, 1999; Lerbinger, 1997); or even its continued existence (Albrecht, 1996; Dressel, 1981; Pauchant & Mitroff, 1992).

Crises not only threaten organizations, they threaten people and property. Loewendick (as cited in Coombs, 1999) notes that the word "threat" is often translated to mean "damage." Damage caused by a crisis may include death or injury to people, facility or property damage, or environmental damage.

The literature describes crises as events that often occur suddenly and without warning (e.g., Barton, 1993; Hermann, 1963, 1972; Holsti, 1978; Phelps, 1986; Seymour & Moore, 2000). The sudden nature of these events makes them difficult to respond to because of the limited time available for making decisions. It is this characteristic that makes it so important for administrators to develop crisis management plans. However, not all crises occur suddenly (Billings,

Milburn, & Schaalman, 1980; Irvine & Millar, 1996; Koovor-Misra, 1995). Each year, hundreds of organizational crises occur that were predictable and that provided organizational leaders with plenty of warning (Irvine & Millar, 1996). Take, for example, hurricanes. While there may be some uncertainty about exactly where a hurricane will hit, officials usually have several days' notice before the storm strikes.

Another common characteristic of crises is that they disrupt the normal operations of an organization. Seymour and Moore (2000) describe crisis as "the disruption of normal patterns of corporate activity by a sudden or overpowering and initially uncontrollable event" (p. 10). Pauchant and Mitroff (1992) also describe crisis in terms of a disruption. In fact, the concept of crisis as a disruption that causes managers to deal with an abnormal set of circumstances seems to cut across all the various definitions.

Given these common characteristics, the following definition is offered: *A campus crisis is an event, often sudden or unexpected, that disrupts the normal operations of the institution or its educational mission and threatens the well-being of personnel, property, financial resources, and/or reputation of the institution.* In a strict sense, a crisis usually affects the entire institution. Power may be out, various processes in the institution may be interrupted, traffic may be diverted, buildings may be evacuated, classes could be cancelled, and the lives of the people in the institution are in some way touched by this event.

It is also important to recognize that there are different levels of crisis. Some crises extend well beyond the campus borders, some are confined to the campus, and others affect only a subset of the campus community. This gives us three levels: (1) disasters, (2) crises, and (3) critical incidents. A *disaster* is an unexpected event that disrupts normal operations of not only the institution but the surrounding community as well. The most obvious events are natural disasters such as hurricanes, earthquakes, and floods, or disasters such as epidemics, large-scale chemical spills, and terrorist attacks. These events overwhelm campus and community resources, and equipment and services that the campus might otherwise rely on might not be available because they are being used to address needs elsewhere in the community.

A *crisis* is an unexpected event that disrupts the entire institution. Everyone in the organization is affected by the situation; classes may be cancelled and the institution closed. The event is localized to the campus and does not spill over into the surrounding community. Resources and other support from the community may be used in the response, but the focus remains on the campus.

A *critical incident* is an event that causes a disruption to part of the campus community. The disruption may affect a department, college, or segment of the campus, but the rest of the institution is able to function without significant interference. However, if a critical incident is not handled well, it may snowball into a full-blown crisis.

What is a full-blown crisis on one campus may be a critical incident at another, depending on factors such as the size of the institution, the type of institution, location (rural vs. urban), and organizational structure. Thus, experts on crisis management caution that there are no turnkey solutions or one-size-fits-all crisis management plans (Mitroff, Pearson, & Harrington, 1996;

Phelps, 1986). Each institution must review its own circumstances, potential threats, and risks, and establish a crisis management system that meets its unique needs.

Crisis Management Process

Before we discuss forming a crisis management team or creating a crisis management plan, we should understand the crisis management process. Crisis management is often thought of in terms of a single set of actions, usually the response effort. Many organizations focus on being able to "respond" without understanding effective crisis management, what goes into preparing a response, and what will be required to resume operations and return the campus or community to some semblance of normalcy. Crisis management is a process rather than a single set of actions. Various authors describe crisis management as a series of stages (e.g, Abent, 1999; Coombs, 1999; Federal Emergency Management Agency (FEMA), 1996; Koovor-Misra, 1995; Mitroff, Pearson et al., 1996; Ogrizek & Guillery, 1999; Pauchant & Mitroff, 1992). Among the more frequently referenced models are Fink's (1986) crisis life cycle; Pauchant and Mitroff's (1992) five-phase model; the FEMA (1996) four-stage model; and the general three-stage model of crisis. By combining the best features of these models, higher education can benefit from a five-phase crisis management process: (1) prevention and mitigation, (2) planning, (3) response, (4) recovery, and (5) learning (see Figure 1.1).

The first phase of this model recognizes that the best system is one that eliminates potential crises or reduces the likelihood they will occur. In the prevention and mitigation phase, administrators identify potential crisis events in their environment and take actions to prevent them from occurring or mitigate their impact. This is the phase that is most often overlooked in the crisis management process (Guth, 1995; Koovor-Misra, 1995; Mitroff, Pearson et al., 1996; Zdziarski, 2001).

Administrators can begin the crisis management process by conducting a thorough assessment of potential threats and risks. (The crisis audit is described in greater detail later in this chapter.) Once they have a clear picture of the events the campus community faces, they can identify ways to reduce the likelihood that these events will occur or limit their impact. *Prevention and mitigation* may take the form of institutional policies and procedures (such as training programs for drivers of passenger vans) or facility modifications (such as the installation of card reader security systems). While institutions undertake many such risk management efforts, they are rarely part of a comprehensive crisis management process.

Recognizing that we cannot prevent all crises from occurring, we move to the *planning* phase. In this phase, administrators make plans for how to respond to the crisis events that are most likely to occur. This involves developing a campus crisis management plan with accompanying protocols to address the various likely events that were identified in phase one. Rather than attempting to plan for every eventuality, it is important to focus on planning the major components of the response and recovery effort.

The third phase is the *response*. This is when you and your crisis management team actually put your plan into operation. Assuming that you have done a good job in phase two, your plan will be activated smoothly: All individuals and departments will have a clear idea of their role in the response effort and the action they should take. Circumstances or issues not specifically addressed in the plan can be evaluated and acted on by the appropriate individual or brought to the crisis team.

Figure 1.1
Crisis Management Process

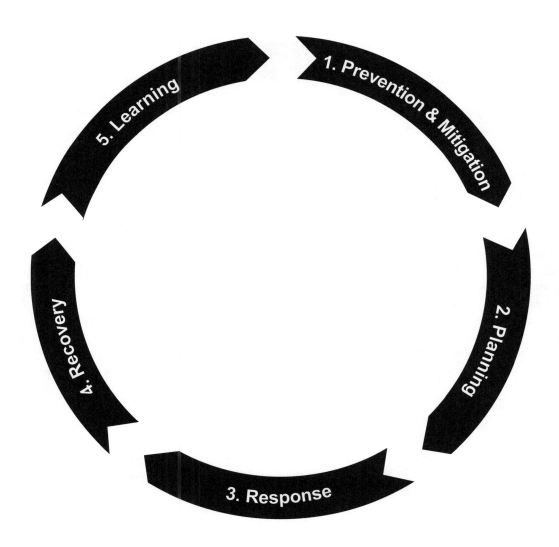

Source: Adapted from FEMA 1996 and Koovor-Misra, 1995.

The fourth phase of the crisis management process is *recovery.* Like the first phase, the recovery phase is often overlooked in planning, although it is the phase that organizations and institutions spend the most time on. While the response may last several hours or even a few days, the recovery goes on for days or weeks, and sometimes months or years. Take, for example, Hurricane Katrina: It will be years before some campuses fully recover from this devastating event. The biggest issue in this phase is resumption of business: How do we resume operations as quickly as possible? Thinking through this phase and developing specific plans to resume operations and bring some semblance of normalcy to the campus is a top priority.

The fifth phase is *learning.* In this phase, the institution should take a close, sometimes painful, look at the crisis: the actions that were taken to prevent it, the preparations that were made, the steps that were followed to contain the crisis and limit the damage, and the plans implemented to recover from the crisis. This is how the institution can improve its crisis management process. This final phase links with the first phase to create a cyclical and interactive process that provides the opportunity for continuous improvement.

Crisis management is not a task or project that has a finite end; it is an ongoing process to keep in mind as we carry out our other duties and responsibilities. We should constantly monitor our environment for potential risks or threats and, if we identify one, be ready to develop ways to prevent the event from occurring or mitigate the impact and revise our response plans as necessary. If the event occurs, we can use our experience with it to further improve our crisis management system.

Stakeholders

Colleges and universities have a variety of stakeholders that can affect or be affected by a crisis. These stakeholders include all the individuals, groups, and organizations that could be affected by a crisis or affect the institution's ability to manage a crisis (Mitroff, Pearson, et al.,1996). In developing a crisis management system for your institution, you must understand who your stakeholders are and what role they will play in various crisis situations.

Crisis situations will involve both internal and external stakeholders (Gonzalez-Herro & Pratt, 1995; Koovor-Misra, 1995; Littleton, 1983; Mitroff, Pearson et al., 1996). Internal stakeholders are individuals, groups, and organizations within the institution. The most obvious internal stakeholders at educational institutions are students (Duncan & Miser, 2000). They are our customers, the people we seek to educate and serve. They are often most vulnerable to a crisis and, therefore, the people we seek to protect.

Student stakeholders belong to different groups that present unique issues or needs in the crisis management process. These include on-campus residents, off-campus students, international students, student athletes, fraternities and sororities, and student government and other student clubs and organizations. For example, the death of an international student would present a number of distinct issues, including interactions with foreign consulates, repatriation of the student's remains, and adherence to cultural and religious customs with which we may not be familiar. Students can also play important roles in responding to a crisis. Student organization leaders are frequently involved in response and recovery efforts and, therefore, should not be forgotten in the prevention and planning phases.

Other internal stakeholders are faculty, staff, and administrators. They, too, represent different subsets or groups. It is useful to consider these stakeholders in terms of positions, offices, departments, or divisions. Again, depending on the nature of the office or department, each of these stakeholders can have a unique impact on the institution's ability to manage a crisis event. See Table 1.1 for a list of potential internal stakeholders.

A variety of external stakeholders may also be affected by a campus crisis. In times of crisis, student affairs staff are often involved in communicating with parents and family members (Duncan & Miser, 2000). The institution may establish toll-free telephone lines or send letters to students' families about crises affecting the campus (Archer, 1992; Duncan & Miser, 2000; Larson, 1994; Lowery & Kibler, 2000; Siegel, 1994).

The media are important external stakeholders (Abent, 1999; Duncan & Miser, 2000; Gonzalez-Herro & Pratt, 1995; Gorman & McKee, 1990; Mitroff, Harrington, & Gai, 1996; Ogrizek & Guillery, 1999; Seymour & Moore, 2000). They are a primary resource for communicating with the community at large (Larson, 1994; Lowery & Kibler, 2000). Some campus crises attract the attention of regional and national media (e.g., Archer, 1992; Hurst, 1999; Larson, 1994; Lowery & Kibler, 2000; Siegel, 1994). In fact, Ogrizek and Guillary (1999) note that some incidents are "neither disasters nor major risk situations, but the media gave them a scale that triggered the outbreak that was without a doubt the root of the crisis" (p. xiv). Managing the institution's response to the media and ensuring that a consistent and accurate message is provided is a very important consideration in crisis management (Coombs, 1999).

Campus crises can involve a number of external agencies and organizations, including local police and fire departments, county and state emergency management agencies, the National Guard, and FEMA (Siegel, 1994). Research has shown that interorganizational coordination enhances the effectiveness of the overall response to crisis events (Mileti & Sorensen, 1987). University administrators need to develop relationships with these external agencies (Lowery & Kibler, 2000) to understand how they will respond in emergencies and how the institution can coordinate its efforts to maximize response effectiveness.

Many police, fire, and medical personnel follow a unified command structure called the Incident Command System (ICS) (FEMA, 1998; Veasey & Morton, 1992). The Department of Homeland Security also has adopted this model. Originally developed to fight wildfires, the ICS includes five major operational components: command, planning, operations, logistics, and finance/administration, and "has the capability to expand or contract to meet the needs of the incident" (FEMA, 1998, p. 1-8). Ultimate authority for managing an emergency rests with the incident commander, initially the senior first-responder at the scene. As a situation grows in size or complexity, command authority transfers to a more senior and more highly qualified incident commander. In most public-sector response operations, the local fire department will assume command and the fire chief will be the incident commander (Veasey & Morton, 1992). Thus, even though an incident may occur on college or university property, the authority for overall management of the crisis may rest with an external emergency agency. That is why it is extremely important for campus administrators to develop strong working relationships with these agencies long before a crisis strikes.

Table 1.1
Internal Stakeholders

Offices, Departments, and Divisions
Governing Board
President
VP Academic Affairs/Provost
VP Administrative Affairs
VP Student Affairs
General Counsel
University Police
University Relations/Public Information Officer
Physical Plant
Environmental Health
Dean of Students
Dean of Faculties
Human Resources
Student Health Services
Student Counseling Services
Employee Assistance
Residence Life
Student Activities
Athletics
International Student Services
Campus Ministers
Students
Faculty

Source: Author compilation.

Table 1.2
External Stakeholders

Offices, Departments, and Agencies
Local Police/Sheriff
State Police
Local Fire Department
State Fire Marshall
Local Hospitals
Local Health Department
State Health Department
Local Mental Health
State Mental Health
Local Emergency Manangement
American Red Cross
Victim Assistance Program
Local Government Officials
State Government Officials
FBI
FEMA
Homeland Security
Alumni Association
Hometown Alumni Clubs
Parents
Local Community Members
Medial: Local, Regional, and National

Source: Author compilation.

Crisis Management Teams

One of the most common systems used to manage a crisis is the crisis management team or unit (Coombs, 1999; Gonzalez-Herro & Pratt, 1995; Griffin & Lewis, 1995; Koovor-Misra, 1995; Littleton, 1983; Mitroff, Harrington et al., 1996; Mitroff, Pearson et al., 1996; Pauchant & Mitroff, 1992; Phelps, 1986; Scott, 1998; Scott, Fukuyama, Dunkel, &Griffin, 1992; Siegel, 1994; Stubbart, 1987). Such a team, considered a best practice in crisis management (Mitroff, Harrington et al., 1996), performs three primary functions: (1) developing and maintaining a crisis management plan; (2) implementing the plan; and (3) dealing with contingencies that may arise that are not addressed by the plan.

To perform these functions, teams should be comprised of people who can access the necessary information and resources to bring to bear on crisis situations. Team members are typically internal stakeholders who have authority over key functional areas within the institution, such as "public safety, physical plant facilities, media relations, student services, and administration" (Siegel, 1994, p. 260). In some cases, major external stakeholders may be included on the team. There is no definitive list of stakeholders who should be on the crisis management team; these decisions depend on the dynamics and culture of each campus.

While the team needs stakeholders who can access needed information and resources in a crisis, it is important to keep the size of the team manageable. A useful method for choosing team members is to conduct a stakeholder analysis. As noted in Table 1.3, stakeholders are identified on four levels of involvement:

> Level 1: Stakeholders whose involvement is essential in virtually all campus crisis situations.
> Level 2: Stakeholders who would be involved in a significant majority of campus crises.
> Level 3: Stakeholders who are periodically or occasionally involved in campus crises.
> Level 4: Stakeholders who are not essential to crisis response efforts or positions that do not exist on your campus or in your community.

Once you complete the analysis, take a look at the stakeholders that are involved at levels 1 and 2. These offices or departments are strong candidates for team membership. On the other hand, level 4 stakeholders would likely be excluded from the team, while those at level 3 might be included in some circumstances.

Table 1.3
Stakeholder Analysis

Internal Stakeholders	Level 1 Represented on Crisis Management Committee or Team	Level 2 Involved in Planning/ Response as Needed	Level 3 Impact/ Consequences of Crisis on This Stakeholder Routinely Considered	Level 4 Not Significant to Crisis Planning/Response or Does Not Exist
President	☐	☐	☐	☐
VP Academic Affairs	☐	☐	☐	☐
VP Administrative Affairs	☐	☐	☐	☐
VP Student Affairs	☐	☐	☐	☐
General Counsel	☐	☐	☐	☐
University Police	☐	☐	☐	☐
University Relations/PIO	☐	☐	☐	☐
Physical Plant	☐	☐	☐	☐
Environmental Health	☐	☐	☐	☐
Dean of Students	☐	☐	☐	☐
Dean of Faculties	☐	☐	☐	☐
Human Resources	☐	☐	☐	☐
Student Health Services	☐	☐	☐	☐
Student Counseling Services	☐	☐	☐	☐
Employee Assistance	☐	☐	☐	☐
Residence Life	☐	☐	☐	☐
Student Activities	☐	☐	☐	☐
Athletics	☐	☐	☐	☐
International Student Services	☐	☐	☐	☐
Campus Ministers	☐	☐	☐	☐
Students	☐	☐	☐	☐
Faculty	☐	☐	☐	☐
Other	☐	☐	☐	☐

Source: Author compilation.

Table 1.3. Continued
Stakeholder Analysis

External Stakeholders	Level 1 Represented on Crisis Management Committee or Team	Level 2 Involved in Planning/ Response as Needed	Level 3 Impact/ Consequences of Crisis on This Stakeholder Routinely Considered	Level 4 Not Significant to Crisis Planning/Response or Does Not Exist
Local Police/Sheriff	☐	☐	☐	☐
State Police	☐	☐	☐	☐
Local Fire Department	☐	☐	☐	☐
State Fire Marshall	☐	☐	☐	☐
Local Hospitals	☐	☐	☐	☐
Local Health Department	☐	☐	☐	☐
State Health Department	☐	☐	☐	☐
Local Emergency Management	☐	☐	☐	☐
American Red Cross	☐	☐	☐	☐
Victim Assistance Program	☐	☐	☐	☐
Local Gov. Officials	☐	☐	☐	☐
State Gov. Officials	☐	☐	☐	☐
FBI	☐	☐	☐	☐
FEMA	☐	☐	☐	☐
Homeland Security	☐	☐	☐	☐
Alumni Association	☐	☐	☐	☐
Hometown Alumni Clubs	☐	☐	☐	☐
Parents	☐	☐	☐	☐
Other	☐	☐	☐	☐

Source: Author compilation.

In a survey of 146 NASPA member institutions that used this stakeholder analysis (Zdziarski, 2001), internal stakeholders with the greatest level of involvement were university police, university relations/public information office, vice president for student affairs, residence life, student counseling services, dean of students, student health services, physical plant, and environmental health and safety. In reviewing this list, people are surprised to learn that the president is not among the top 10 stakeholders. The actual ranking for the president in this study was 13th, but the ranking is less important than the point it illustrates: Although the president is informed and involved in most campus crises, he or she may not necessarily be directly involved on the crisis management team. This depends on the president's personal style and the culture of the institution, but the president usually delegates the direction of the crisis management team to a senior administrator. This administrator has the authority to make routine decisions regarding the institutional response, while keeping the president apprised of the situation and seeking his or her guidance on major issues.

Another position that is conspicuously absent from the top 10 is the general counsel, who ranks 12th. While the legal implications of a crisis situation are important, they should not be the primary force driving institutional decisions in crisis response. It is easy to recognize actions that are taken to protect the institution from legal liability and these decisions often create distrust and generate animosity toward the institution. Conversely, decisions or actions that are taken with the best interests of those affected in mind are also easily recognized, demonstrate a level of compassion on the part of the organization, and generate a positive impression of the institution. In "responding from the heart," administrators may weigh the legal implications, but their course of action will be based on the right thing to do.

The specific makeup of your crisis management team will depend on the culture and dynamics of your campus. After you have conducted a stakeholder analysis to identify possible team members, you can invite them to participate. Sometimes membership will be designated by supervisors; sometimes people will volunteer. How people become members is less important than ensuring that you have the right combination of people on your team.

Conducting a Crisis Audit

The first step in developing a crisis management plan is to conduct a crisis audit—a systematic examination of the risks and threats the organization faces in both its internal and external environments (Littleton, 1983). In the audit, the organization attempts to identify the various crisis events it might face and the impact these events might have on the organization. Administrators will want to focus their planning efforts on crisis events with the highest probability of occurring and the greatest potential impact on the institution. However, the planners should not limit their preparations to high-probability, high-impact events. While a particular crisis might have a low probability of occurring, its devastating effects should be considered when developing organizational protocols (Mitroff, Pearson et al., 1996).

Hundreds of different crisis events could take place on a college campus, and it is not practical or possible to prepare a response to all of them. Instead, organizations focus on developing protocols for the major types of crisis. The literature suggests that crisis events can be grouped in relatively distinct sets or clusters, often referred to as a "crisis typology" (Coombs, 1999; Koovor-Misra, 1995; Mitroff, Pearson et al., 1996; Pauchant & Mitroff, 1992).

In a study that sought to identify institutional preparedness to respond to campus crises (Zdziarski, 2001), I proposed a crisis typology for higher education. This typology identifies four major types of campus crises: natural, facility, criminal, and human. Natural crises include tornados, floods, hurricanes, and earthquakes. Facility crises include fires, explosions, chemical leaks, loss of utilities, loss of computer data, and evacuation of buildings or campus. Criminal events include sexual assaults/batteries, sexual harassment, homicides, assaults, hate crimes, burglary/robbery, domestic abuse, vandalism, terrorist threat, and kidnapping/abduction. Human crises include injuries, deaths (including suicide and alcohol/drug overdose), emotional/psychological crises, infectious disease, racial incidents, campus disturbance/demonstration, and missing persons. A crisis audit worksheet based on this typology is provided in Table 1.4.

Key campus stakeholders should be involved in the crisis audit. These stakeholders might include representatives from campus law enforcement, campus health care and counseling services, residence life, academic affairs, and physical plant. If a crisis management team exists, team members are a good choice to conduct the audit. Some experts (Mitroff, Pearson et al., 1996; Stubbart, 1987) suggest that involving individuals outside the organization can sometimes be effective, as it gives the process a different perspective and avoids the potential of overlooking potential risks that insiders might fail to recognize.

Once you assemble your group of relevant stakeholders, the objective is to identify the crisis events your institution is likely to face and the impact they might have. Using the crisis audit worksheet, participants rate the probability that each event will occur on your campus from 1 to 5, where 1 is least likely to occur and 5 is most likely to occur. They also rate the potential impact of each event from 1 to 5, where 1 is minor impact and 5 is severe impact. These two ratings are combined to get an overall rating for each crisis event. Participants should complete the process individually and then as a group. It is important to note that the list of potential crisis events is by no means exhaustive; it is intended as a starting point to assess your campus's vulnerability. Participants should be encouraged to add any crisis events they believe are relevant to your campus.

Table 1.4
Campus Crisis Audit Worksheet

Type of Crisis	Crisis Potential		
	Probability of Occuring	Campus Impact	Total
Natural			
Tornado			
Hurricane			
Earthquake			
Flood			
Severe Weather			
Other			
Facility			
Fire			
Explosion			
Chemical Leak			
Evacuation of Campus			
Evacuation of Buildings			
Corruption/Loss of Computer Files			
Loss of Utilities (e.g., electricity, A//C, telephone)			
Other			
Criminal			
Homicide			
Assault			
Sexual Assault/Rape			
Sexual Harassment			
Domestic Abuse			
Burglary/Robbery			
Kidnapping/Abduction			
Hate Crime			
Terrorist Threat			
Vandalism			
Other			
Human			
Student Death			
Faculty/Staff Death			
Student Injury			
Faculty/Staff Injury			
Suicide			
Emotional/Psychological Crisis			
Missing Person			
Alcohol/Drug Overdose			
Infectious Disease			
Racial Incident			
Campus Disturbance/Demonstration			
Other			

Source: Author compilation.

In the discussion comparing individual responses, participants should consider the likelihood and impact of each event, as well as the following questions:

- Does the impact of the crisis event depend on the particular circumstances of the incident?

- If so, what are these circumstances, and how can we prevent or mitigate them?

- What key resources are essential to responding to particular events?

- What external agencies or groups might respond to particular types of crisis events?

Through this discussion, participants will gain insight into the intricacies of the various crisis events and how they might play out on their campus. Planning and preparing for every kind of crisis is not realistic or feasible; the crisis audit enables institutions to set priorities for planning. Minimally, the institution should identify a potential crisis event in each cluster (natural, facility, criminal, and human) and develop protocols for dealing with each one.

The crisis audit is not a one-time exercise; auditing the organization's environment should be an ongoing process, with a formal audit conducted annually (Mitroff, Pearson et al., 1996). Many institutions maintain relevant data that can be used in the crisis auditing process. Statistical data from campus safety and security, health care services, human resources, student conduct, and counseling centers, as well as records from past responses to crises can be an invaluable aid to the process.

Crisis Management Plans

The foundation of any crisis management system is a written plan that provides a clear basis from which everyone in the institution can operate in the event of a crisis. The plan includes instructions for when and how it should be implemented, who will be in charge, and what actions will be taken. A written plan lends continuity and structure to your crisis management system and enables you to train people to carry it out.

Despite the obvious advantages, studies have shown that only about half of the organizations have a written crisis management plan (Pauchant & Mitroff, 1992). In a survey of public relations professionals conducted by David W. Guth (1995), only 56.9% of organizations had written crisis plans. 83.8% of the practitioners at for-profit organizations, 68.5% at not-for-profit organizations, and 62.5% at government organizations indicated that they had a written crisis management plan.

Higher education appears to fare slightly better. In a regional study of institutions in the Southeast, 85% of the respondents indicated that crisis response staff had written procedures, protocols, or policies to follow (Scott, 1999). Similar results were obtained in a national study of NASPA member institutions, which indicated that 88.4% of the institutions surveyed had some type of written crisis management plan (Zdziarski, 2001).

Crisis management plans may exist at various levels within an institution of higher education. In a well-developed crisis management system, organizational units will have their own crisis management plans. For example, a system might include an institutional plan supplemented by division plans (e.g., Academic Affairs, Student Affairs, Finance and Administration) that are in turn supplemented by college or department plans. Each of these plans supports the larger unit or institutional plan to create an integrated system for responding to a crisis.

Whether you are developing a new plan or revising an old one, it may be helpful to review plans created by other institutions. Many institutional or unit crisis management plans are available on the Internet. You might also contact your colleagues at comparable institutions and ask them to share their crisis management plan. If you are creating a new plan, reviewing plans from other institutions can give you a good sense of what a plan looks like and how others have approached some of the issues and challenges you may be facing. If you are revising your plan, reviewing plans from other institutions may help you identify ideas or approaches.

Although reviewing plans from other institutions can be beneficial, you can't just adopt another institution's plan without modifying it to fit your needs.

A good crisis management plan includes two major components: a basic plan and crisis protocols. The *basic plan* outlines the general process the institution or unit will go through in a crisis situation, regardless of the type of crisis. A basic plan should identify the purpose of the plan, who has the authority to activate it, and the specific action steps.

In the purpose statement, the institution or unit defines what it considers a crisis. Not all campuses will define "crisis" the same way; in this statement, the organization describes the circumstances under which the plan will be activated. The level of the event (critical incident, crisis, or disaster) the plan is designed to address may vary depending on whether it is a departmental, college, divisional, or institutional plan.

The plan identifies the individual or group that has the authority to activate it. This person or group must be must be accessible, must be able to make decisions and operate under pressure, and must have appropriate training and experience in dealing with crisis events. Depending on the campus, this authority could be one person or a group of people who share the responsibility for being on call.

How is the on-call staff member contacted when a crisis situation arises? Is he or she notified directly or through some other individual or office? Is this person or office available after hours and on weekends or holidays? How is the campus community informed of this process? These are all important considerations in developing your basic crisis management plan.

To ensure the plan's effectiveness, you need a simple and consistent mechanism for activating it. Some campuses use the university police department as the primary mechanism for activating their plan, because the police are a natural contact for the campus community when a crisis occurs. On many campuses, the police are available 24 hours a day, seven days a week. Or it may be possible to receive notification of a crisis event from security personnel or off-campus agencies. The advantage of this approach is that once the dispatcher has notified the appropriate emergency personnel, he or she can notify university staff/administrators to activate the crisis management plan. Whether the plan is activated through a dispatcher or by members of the campus community, the university staff/administrators identified as first responders are usually notified by a cell phone, pager, or phone tree system.

Finally, your plan must outline a relatively consistent set of actions that will be taken in any crisis situation. These steps might identify how other crisis team members are deployed, the basic roles of these team members, what resources will be used, and how decisions will be made and communicated.

The basic plan is the overall template for how the institution or unit will respond to a crisis. It should be relatively simple and concise, so it can be easily communicated and understood by team members and by the campus community.

Along with basic plans, organizations need to develop *crisis protocols* to address specific types of situations that are likely to occur and identify actions and resources needed to respond to them. This is where the crisis audit really comes into play. Your audit should have identified a representative crisis event for each of the clusters (natural, facility, criminal, and human). You also should have prepared a "crisis portfolio" (Mitroff, Harrington, & Gai, 1996; Mitroff, Pearson et al., 1996; Pauchant & Mitroff, 1992) that includes a protocol for that event. It is not possible to develop a protocol for every conceivable type of crisis, and the actions and resources needed to respond to a crisis within each crisis type are often very similar. Thus, focusing on the key crisis events identified in your audit should provide you with a solid portfolio of protocols to respond to almost any crisis event.

Crisis protocols should be simple and concise. They often take the form of checklists that provide important memory triggers to action steps that need to be taken, resources that should be used, and issues that should be considered. Protocols should provide enough information to guide your response but be simple enough that they can be implemented with a brief review. Remember that every crisis event is unique; contingencies that are not covered in your protocol will be addressed by the crisis management team.

Simply *having* a written plan and crisis protocols is not enough; to be well prepared, you should review and update them regularly. In the event of a crisis, the organization needs current and accurate information. Best practices suggest an annual review.

Training

In addition to an updated plan, you'll need team members who are properly trained to implement it. People need to know specifically what their roles are and what will be expected of them during a crisis event. Tabletop exercises and crisis simulations are effective training methods. In a tabletop exercise, team members are presented with a crisis scenario and asked to describe how they would respond. This approach allows team members to process situations collectively, considering situations from multiple perspectives and in various roles. Tabletop exercises are a good way to test new protocols and identify gaps in the organization's response. A crisis simulation is a full-scale run-through of a crisis event. Much like a role-play, it involves the use of volunteers as "victims" and the activation of all agencies and resources that would respond to such an event. Simulation exercises require extensive coordination and planning, but they provide the most realistic exposure to what a crisis situation will be like and the best test of whether the plans and protocols will be effective.

Conclusion

Crisis management is an essential role of college and university administrators. Regardless of the size, type, or nature of the institution, crises can and will occur. This chapter has focused on the mechanics of developing an effective and comprehensive crisis management system in an institution of higher education. However, the framework of teams, plans, and protocols is just the skeleton of the crisis management system. The following chapters will fill in this framework and explore the personal aspects of crisis response—a response that isn't always outlined in procedures and protocols but focuses on doing the right thing for the people who are involved in the crisis. A response that comes from the heart.

References

Abent, R. (1999). *Managing in time of crisis.* NASPA NetResults. [Online serial] Available: www.naspa.org/Results/pubrelat/managing.html. Accessed: November 30, 1999.

Albrecht, S. (1996). *Crisis management for corporate self-defense: How to protect your organization in a crisis...how to stop a crisis before it starts.* New York: American Management Association.

Archer, J. (1992). *Campus in crisis: Coping with fear and panic related to serial murders.* Journal of Counseling and Development, 71, 96–100.

Auerbach, S. M., & Kilmann, P. R. (1977). *Crisis intervention: A review of outcome research.* Psychological Bulletin, 84(6), 1189–1217.

Barton, L. (1993). *Crisis in organizations: Managing and communicating in the heat of chaos.* Cincinnati, OH: South-Western Publishing.

Billings, R. S., Milburn, T. W., & Schaalman, M. L. (1980). *A model of crisis perception: A theoretical and empirical analysis.* Administrative Science Quarterly, 25, 300–316.

Cleary, H., & Cleary, C. (2001). *What Jeanne didn't know.* Retrieved December 9, 2005, from http://securityoncampus.org/aboutsoc/didntknow.html.

Coombs, W. T. (1999). *Ongoing crisis communication: Planning, managing, and responding (Vol. 2).* Thousand Oaks, CA: Sage.

Dressel, P. L. (1981). *Administrative leadership: Effective and responsive decision making in higher education.* San Francisco: Jossey-Bass.

Duncan, M. A., & Miser, K. M. (2000). *Dealing with campus crisis.* In M. J. Barr & M. K.

Desler & Associates (Eds.), *Handbook of student affairs administration* (2nd ed., pp. 453–473). San Francisco: Jossey-Bass.

Federal Emergency Management Agency (FEMA). (1996). *State and local guide (SLG 101): Guide for all-hazard emergency operations planning.* [Online] Available: www.fema.gov/pte/gaheop.htm.

FEMA. (1998). *Basic incident command system* (IS 195). [Online] Available: www.fema.gov/emi/is1951st.htm.

Fink, S. (1986). *Crisis management: Planning for the inevitable.* New York: American Management Association.

Gonzalez-Herro, A., & Pratt, C. B. (1995). *How to manage a crisis before—or whenever—it hits.* Public Relations Quarterly, 40(1), 25–29.

Gorman, L., & McKee, K. D. (1990). *Disaster and its aftermath. HR Magazine* (Spring), 54–58.

Griffin, W. D., & Lewis, L. A. (1995, October). *The trauma response team: An institutional response to crisis.* ACPA Commission VII Counseling and Psychological Services, 22(2), 3–4.

Guth, D. W. (1995). *Organizational crisis experience and public relations roles.* Public Relations Review, 21(2), 123–136.

Hermann, C. F. (1963). *Some consequences of crisis which limit the viability of organizations.* Administrative Science Quarterly, 8, 61–82.

Hermann, C. F. (1972). *Threat, time and surprise: A simulation of international crises.* In C. F. Hermann (Ed.), International crises: Insights from behavioral research (pp. 187–211). New York: Free Press.

Holsti, O. R. (1978). *Limitations of cognitive abilities in the face of crisis.* In C. F. Smart & W. T. Stansbury (Eds.), *Studies in crisis management* (pp. 39–55). Toronto: Butterworth & Company.
Hurst, J. C. (1999). *The Mathew Sheppard tragedy: Management of a crisis.* About Campus, 4(3), 5–11.

Irvine, R. B., & Millar, D. P. (1996). *Debunking the stereotypes of crisis management: The nature of business crisis in the 1990s.* Institute for Crisis Management. [Online] Available: www.crisis-experts.com/debunking_main.htm.

Koovor-Misra, S. (1995). *A multidimensional approach to crisis preparation for technical organizations: Some critical factors.* Technological Forecasting and Social Change, 48, 143–160.
Larson, W. A. (1994). *When crisis strikes on campus.* Washington, D.C.: Council for the Advancement and Support of Education.

Lerbinger, O. (1997). *The crisis manager: Facing risk and responsibility.* Mahwah, NJ: Lawrence Erlbaum Associates.

Levitt, A. M. (1997). *Disaster planning and recovery: A guide for facility professionals.* New York: John Wiley & Sons.

Littleton, R. F. (1983). *Crisis management: A team approach.* New York: American Management Association.

Lowery, J. W., & Kibler, B. (2000). *Bonfire: Tragedy and tradition.* About Campus, 5(3), 20–25.
May 4 Task Force. (1996). *Chronology of events: Kent State: May 1–4, 1970.* Retrieved December 11, 2005, from http://dept.kent.edu/may4/chrono.html

Mileti, D. S., & Sorensen, J. H. (1987). *Determinants of organizational effectiveness in responding to low probability catastrophic events.* Columbia Journal of World Business, 22, 13–21.
Mitroff, I. I., Harrington, L. K., & Gai, E. (1996). *Thinking about the unthinkable.* Across the Board, 33(8), 44–48.

Mitroff, I. I., Pearson, C. M., & Harrington, L. K. (1996). *The essential guide to managing corporate crisis: A step-by-step handbook for surviving major catastrophes.* New York: Oxford University Press.

Ogrizek, M., & Guillery, J.-M. (1999). *Communicating in crisis: A theoretical and practical guide to crisis management* (H. Kimball-Brooke & R. Z. Brooke, Trans.). New York: Aldine De Gruyter.

Pauchant, T. C., & Mitroff, I. I. (1992). *Transforming the crisis-prone organization: Preventing individual, organizational, and environmental tragedies.* San Francisco: Jossey-Bass.

Phelps, N. L. (1986). *Setting up a crisis recovery plan. Journal of Business Strategy, 6*(4), 5–11.
Rollo, J. M. (1999). *Historical overview of campus trauma.* Paper presented at the Institute for Crisis Management in Higher Education, University of Florida, Gainesville, FL.

Scott, J. E. (1998). *Crisis management in student affairs: The Florida murders.* ACUHO-I Talking Stick, 16(2), 13–14.

Scott, J. E. (1999). [Crisis management survey]. Unpublished raw data.

Scott, J. E., Fukuyama, M. A., Dunkel, N. W., & Griffin, W. D. (1992). *The trauma response team: Preparing staff to respond to student death.* NASPA Journal, 29(3), 230–237.

Seymour, M., & Moore, S. (2000). *Effective crisis management: Worldwide principles and practice.* London: Cassell.

Siegel, D. (1994). *Campuses respond to violent tragedy.* Phoenix: Oryx Press.

Stubbart, C. I. (1987). *Improving the quality of crisis thinking.* Columbia Journal of World Business, 22, 89–99.

Veasey, D. A., & Morton, C. H. (1992). *Incident command system.* In L. P. Andrews (Ed.), *Emergency responder training manual for the hazardous materials technician* (pp. 28–42). New York: Van Nostrand Reinhold.

Zdziarski, E. L. (2001). *Institutional preparedness to respond to campus crises as perceived by student affairs administrators in selected NASPA member institutions.* (Doctoral dissertation, Texas A&M University, 2001). Dissertation Abstracts International, 62, 3714.

Chapter 2

Establishing a Crisis Response Team: Moving from Institutional to Personal Response

Brent G. Paterson

This chapter is based on the author's personal experience creating and coordinating crisis response teams at Texas A&M University and Illinois State University. While some of the information is specific to these institutions, readers are welcome to adapt the information to their campuses.

In chapter 1, Gene Zdziarski discussed crisis management plans and teams at the institutional level. Institutional plans tend to be detailed, written documents that describe procedures for typical types of emergencies at a college or university: building fire, natural disaster (hurricane, tornado, earthquake, flood), terrorist threat or action, or hazardous material spill. These plans usually are developed by campus health and safety offices, and they tend to involve elaborate hierarchical decision-making matrixes with the college or university president at the top. Such plans often neglect the human factor—responding to the emotional and psychological effects of a crisis on students and their families. It is assumed that student affairs will take care of these needs. As many student affairs divisions have discovered, careful planning and practice are necessary to appropriately respond to a critical incident, crisis, or disaster involving students.

Definition of a Crisis

This chapter focuses on student affairs' response to a crisis, so the definition of "crisis" may differ from that used in a campus crisis plan. The definition should be broad enough to cover unexpected situations (e.g., a plane crash) but should apply specifically to a crisis in which student affairs will respond rather than a "bricks and mortar" crisis that does not affect students. Bornstein and Wilson (2004) define a crisis on campus as "an unexpected event that causes increased stress to the institution's community, or some part of that community." In chapter 1, Zdziarski differentiates among a critical incident, a crisis, and a disaster: A critical incident affects a subset of the campus community; a crisis affects the whole campus community and disrupts normal activities; and a disaster affects not only the campus community but also the surrounding community.

In practice, though, the three terms are used interchangeably. At Illinois State University (ISU), student affairs defines a critical incident as "an adverse event that causes or has the potential to cause harm to an individual student, group of students, or the university and requires immediate response from the Division of Student Affairs" (*Critical Incident Response Team Training Manual*, 2003). Universities usually further define a critical incident/crisis by listing typical incidents addressed by a student affairs crisis response team. Such incidents commonly include death of a student on or off campus, life-threatening injury or illness, communicable disease, fire/explosion or significant damage to a campus building or student residence, missing person, sexual assault, riot/campus disruption, and natural disaster (*Trauma Response Team,* 2005; Mamarchev, Paterson, & Whipple, 2002). In this chapter, the word "crisis" is used in its generic form to include critical incidents and disasters.

Considerations for Establishing a Student Affairs Crisis Response Team

Formal crisis response plans and crisis response teams in student affairs divisions are recent developments. Residence halls have always had protocols and procedures for incidents in the halls, but incidents occurring outside the residence halls or those that require intervention by the vice president's office have usually been handled informally. The response depended on the personality and interest of the senior student affairs officer and the relationships he or she had with campus and community police departments and the community fire department. This informal approach may still work at small colleges in small communities, but most student affairs divisions need a crisis plan and team. Unfortunately, crisis plans and crisis response teams are often created in response to an incident.

As the newly appointed director of student life at Texas A&M University, I was charged with developing a division crisis response plan. The vice president for student affairs appointed a task force that included the director of residence life, the director of student activities, and me to work together on the plan. Our assignment was in response to a student death at a freshman orientation camp. An investigation of the incident had recommended a review of department protocols dealing with life-threatening injuries, specifically those that addressed communication and authority issues when the vice president cannot be reached (Reber, 1995).

As the task group began to grapple with its charge, it was evident that we needed to address issues beyond simply determining the best thing to do. First, we needed to know the expectations of the vice president. Whom did he expect to respond to a crisis? Would he be willing to delegate decision making in those situations? How low in the chain of command was too low? Second, there were political issues. Residence life staff do not want staff from student life or student activities involved in what happens in the residence hall. Student activities divisions believe that student organizations are their responsibility. Academic departments consider laboratories their domain. How would academic departments react if student affairs staff responded to a student injured in a lab accident? We have a counseling service—should they be the responders? After all, counselors are trained in responding to emotional trauma. Third, relationships with the university police would be critical to the success of a crisis response team, and other relationships would also need to be developed, in the university and in the community. Fourth, the serious injury or death of a student always triggers the fear of a lawsuit. Our task force would have to explore the concerns of the university counsel regarding crisis response.

Role of a Student Affairs Crisis Response Team

As we explored these issues, we defined the purpose of what would become known as the Critical Incident Response Team (CIRT). Student affairs staff would respond to critical incidents in the local area. Staff would also serve as the university contact when students are involved in critical incidents away from the College Station campus. The role of staff in responding to a critical incident would be as follows:

1. To coordinate the university's response to critical incidents involving students, paying special attention to the safety and security needs of members of the university community.

2. To offer counseling, guidance, and appropriate support to members of the university community, their families, and university caregivers.

3. To use critical incidents, when appropriate, as "teachable moments" to enhance the quality of life for all those touched by the incident. (*Critical Incident Response Team*, 2005)

As these guidelines indicate, the focus of the student affairs crisis response is on the student and his or her family; this focus allows student affairs to support the efforts of emergency response personnel without interfering. We found that emergency response personnel welcomed the assistance of student affairs staff in responding to the emotional needs of affected students. Initially, there was some questioning: Who are you, and why are you here? But after a little education of the police, fire departments, and emergency room staff at local hospitals, the calls for assistance came pouring in.

The student affairs crisis response plan and team should be a component of the larger institutional crisis management plan, and the larger plan should define the role of the student affairs crisis response team in terms of other responders. The leader of the student affairs team should be a member of the institutional crisis management team and should participate in meetings, drills, and real-life incident response. As noted earlier, institutional crisis response plans tend to focus on physical structures and property; they rarely touch on the emotional needs of students affected by a crisis.

While the task force was developing plans for a student affairs crisis response plan, a real crisis hit the university. One morning, I received a call from the university police saying that there had been a murder and kidnapping earlier that morning. A student had broken into an off-campus duplex, killing one student and kidnapping another. We didn't have a plan in place, so I gathered as much information as I could about the situation from the police, then asked my assistant to check the records for information on the students involved. I told the vice president for student affairs what I knew. As the details of the incident emerged, we discovered that the kidnapped student was safe, but we did not know how to contact her. The alleged murderer/kidnapper was in police custody. The parents of the murder victim lived in England—was it my responsibility to call them? It was at this point that we clarified that the police are the first contact with the family of a victim. We would follow up with the family after the police had made contact.

We learned some valuable lessons from this incident, which were not addressed in the campus crisis plan. Obviously, student affairs needed to be involved in responding to such an incident. Our first concern was for the kidnapped student. With the assistance of the police, we were able to get word to her that the university was concerned about her well-being: Services were available through student counseling; her professors were notified that she would be missing class for a few days; and we let her know that arrangements could be made for her to live on campus. There was nothing we could or should do for the student accused of murder, but a few days after the incident, we learned that he had a sister who was also enrolled at the university. She needed our assistance as much as the student who had been kidnapped.

We also discovered that responding to such incidents can be personal. My assistant attended the same church as the victim and knew her. My assistant's husband worked at a local business that also employed the murderer; in fact, her husband had been working with him a few hours before the incident. At the time, I was not sensitive to the stress I was placing on her by asking her to respond to a crisis in which she had a personal connection.

With a renewed sense of urgency, the task force went to work on a plan for crisis response in student affairs. We shifted our efforts to defining protocols and determining who would represent the division in such incidents. When the department of student life was established, it was envisioned as a dean of students office (campus politics confined the use of the "dean" title to directors of academic colleges). With this vision, it seemed logical that the new department would have responsibility for coordinating the crisis response for the division of student affairs. This meant working closely with other departments in the division, especially residence life and student activities, in responding to incidents. Staff in these departments had unique relationships with students living in the halls and those involved in student organizations. Cooperation would be essential for an appropriate response. In addition, relationships would need to be strengthened with the student counseling service, university police, university health and safety office, and international student office.

It was obvious to me after responding to the murder/kidnapping that a degree in student affairs was not adequate preparation for crisis response. In some ways, I had an advantage, because my master's degree is in counseling. However, responding to a crisis does not allow for a one-on-one counseling session. We needed to form a team to respond to crisis situations and that team would need training. It was determined that we would use senior staff in the department of student life to serve on what would be called the Critical Incident Response Team (CIRT). This group of four (director, associate director, two assistant directors) would develop the protocols for responding to a crisis and develop the relationships with key constituencies that would ensure the team's success.

Protocols

I believe in the KISS (keep it simple, stupid) philosophy. My experience with the student murder/kidnapping showed that there would not be time in a crisis to refer to an extensive manual with detailed procedures. I also knew that no manual could anticipate every situation. Thus, we designed a procedures outline that contained the basics and could be adapted to any crisis situation. This approach has worked well for us over the years and has been adopted by other campuses.

Our approach involves eight steps:

Step 1. University police are notified of a crisis affecting a university student. _ incident may be on or off campus.

Step 2. University police notify the Critical Incident Response Team on-call person via the CIRT pager. This person gathers necessary information on the situation and the student(s) affected, then contacts appropriate staff/individuals, including the vice president for student affairs. If the situation warrants, the CIRT on-call person proceeds immediately to the site of the incident or to the hospital. The on-call person may request assistance from other CIRT members at the site of the incident, the hospital, or other locations. The on-call person works with media relations to coordinate any press releases or contact with the media.

Step 3. The CIRT on-call person verifies that police, hospital, coroner, or other appropriate personnel have contacted the family of the affected student. A member of the CIRT or the vice president for student affairs officially contacts the family to offer appropriate support from the university. The on-call person verifies that contact has been made with roommate(s), significant other/partner, and brother or sister (if a university student). The on-call person may elicit assistance from other CIRT members or other university staff in making these contacts. Residence life staff may be used to contact individuals in residence halls. When contact is made, affected individuals should be informed of available services, such as student counseling.

Step 4. If the situation warrants, a campus visit is arranged for the family. An escort is arranged for them, and a CIRT member makes arrangements to meet any family needs, as appropriate.

Step 5. The family meets with appropriate university administrators, police officers, the campus minister (if desired), and other officials as requested or needed.

Step 6. The CIRT meets to plan any appropriate follow-up activities.

Step 7. The CIRT meets to debrief, evaluate the procedures followed, and make improvements for the future.

Step 8. As appropriate, individuals who are involved in responding to critical incidents should participate in a Critical Incident Stress Management program.

There is no time line for the eight steps. Some incidents may require only a few hours, while others will involve weeks or even months of follow-up. An incident may require only the response of the CIRT on-call person; a major crisis will consume all available resources.

In developing protocols, the question of authority emerges. The members of the CIRT need to be empowered to make decisions on behalf of the division of student affairs, and sometimes the university, in responding to a crisis. The CIRT cannot contact the vice president for student affairs every time a new issue arises during a crisis. The issue may be as simple as taking a student to ie store to purchase clothing because his or her clothes were lost in a fire or arranging for on-campus housing and a temporary meal plan.

There is a special role for the vice president for student affairs in crisis response. He or she is the communication link to the president and other vice presidents. His or her authority and relationships are important when additional resources are needed to respond to a crisis. The vice president can be a spokesperson for the division or the university when media relations determines that the public should hear an administrator's voice. He or she can meet with affected students and their families after the initial crisis response. The vice president also can be the person who determines how response to a crisis fits in with other priorities.

The Crisis Response Team

The structure and name of the crisis response team vary greatly by institution. Some campuses have a dean on duty; in this scenario, a staff member in the dean of students office is always on call to respond to emergencies. At Illinois State, the CIRT includes directors in the division of student affairs as well as staff in the office of the vice president for student affairs. A member of the CIRT carries a pager and is on call 24 hours a day for a weeklong shift. At Bowling Green State University, the team is referred to as COPES (Coordinator of Personal Emergency Services). A designated staff person is on call 24/7 to respond to student emergencies or crises (Mamarchev et al., 2002). The University of Florida has the Trauma Response Team (*Trauma Response Team*, 2005). Whatever structure or title is used, the basic goal is the same: assisting students in times of crisis.

The size of a crisis response team will differ by institutional size and culture. The original CIRT at Texas A&M had four members. There were some distinct advantages in having such a small group. The four of us worked closely every day in the same office suite, so it was easy to share information. This setup also permitted us to involve clerical staff in appropriate ways.
The arrangement worked extremely well for the first four years. We trusted each other's judgment and shared insights to determine the best response to a situation. When a larger crisis occurred, we worked as a team, dividing responsibilities and communicating with each other and those who had a need to know.

The bonfire incident in November 1999 changed our thinking about the membership of the CIRT. Texas A&M University students had built a bonfire since 1909 to demonstrate their "burning desire" to defeat their archrival the University of Texas at football. This was no ordinary pep rally bonfire. It was a massive effort by students to construct a 59-foot structure of wedding cake design. Shortly after 2:30 a.m. on November 18, 1999, the logs that made up the near-complete structure crashed to the ground, killing 12 students and seriously injuring 27 other students. This large-scale incident consumed all available resources of the CIRT and the university. CIRT members were on the scene within minutes, and everyone was involved in crisis response for the next 24 hours. The following days and weeks involved long hours attempting to keep regular work going while attending to the needs of the families of the students who died in the accident and the other students who were seriously injured. In fact, these efforts consumed the remainder of the academic year. CIRT members were overwhelmed, so we added new members to help distribute the workload.

At ISU, the CIRT has nine members. The team includes the division senior leadership team (vice president, associate vice president, assistant vice president, dean of students, and assistant to the vice president), senior leadership in the dean of students office (assistant dean of students, associate dean of students, and dean of students), and the director of student counseling services. Because these individuals are spread out around the campus, communication among CIRT members does not flow easily. Fortunately, ISU does not experience as many critical incidents as Texas A&M does, mainly because it is less than half the size (20,000 compared with 44,000). The Texas A&M CIRT established excellent working relationships with police and fire departments and local hospitals. Because major incidents at ISU are significantly fewer, it has been more difficult to build these relationships. The agencies have not been able to see how CIRT can be of assistance to them. Also affecting the relationships is the implementation of the Health Insurance Portability and Accountability Act (HIPAA). The standards for privacy of medical records in HIPAA have caused hospitals and emergency responders to be very concerned about sharing any medical information about a student without the student's consent.

One of my concerns about the response system at ISU is that we have not had enough practice. While tabletop exercises are valuable teaching tools, the team needs to experience responding to a crisis and learning from the experience. I made this statement at a monthly CIRT meeting and, less than a week later, an off-campus apartment complex was destroyed by a fire. Fortunately, no tenants were injured. We had the real-world experience that permitted us to strengthen relationships with university departments, emergency response agencies, and community agencies.

In determining the membership of a crisis response team, it is important to consider the skill set of the individuals. Each one should have an understanding of the university administrative structure. A crisis team member must understand who needs information about the crisis, what they should know, and when they should know it. The team member also must understand when decisions are outside his or her scope of authority and who has such authority. Team members need to have "project manager skills": the ability to sort, prioritize, communicate, and track.

Personality and character are important. The individual must exude empathy, have confidence in his or her ability to handle a crisis situation, be level-headed, and be mentally and emotionally strong. He or she must be able to work with ambiguity and be willing to ask for assistance, both professionally and personally. It is important that the individual is willing to sin bravely.

What is meant by "sinning bravely"? Fear of a lawsuit or concern for the university's image should not prevent a crisis team member from doing the right thing. One of the first incidents to which I responded as a CIRT member involved a student who had been run over by a university bus. The student was training for a bike race on campus streets. As he turned a corner, a university bus pulled out in front of him, and his bike slid under the rear wheels of the bus. The student suffered severe head injuries, a broken jaw, broken ribs, a punctured lung, and shattered bones in his legs. It was clear to me that my role was to be there to express concern for the welfare of the student on behalf of the university and to help in appropriate ways, not to be concerned about a potential lawsuit or the university's image.

I visited with the student's father on several occasions during the 10 weeks the student remained in a coma and the additional weeks he was in the hospital. Mostly, we talked about the student's love for the university, his friends who came to visit, his girlfriend, and the medical progress or disappointment of the day. It was important to the father that the university cared about his son. When the discussion strayed to specific issues about the accident, I told the father that he would need to speak to the appropriate office or administrator to get answers to his questions. I could honestly say that I did not know the answers and had not involved myself in that way. However, I was more than willing to arrange for the father to meet with the appropriate person or attempt to gather the information he was seeking.

(The student made a slow but amazing recovery. Following years of rehabilitation, he completed the MS 150, a 150-mile bicycle ride from Houston to Austin benefiting the Multiple Sclerosis Society. Eight years after the accident, he graduated from the university with a bachelor's degree and enrolled in graduate school at another university.)

In summary, sinning bravely involves understanding that the university may need to take a public stance, but the crisis team should not let this stance interfere with doing the right thing for the affected students and their families. Lawsuits will happen; don't take them personally. The lawsuit will be focused on the incidents, not your response to the affected students. Make friendly referrals. Connect the affected students and their families with the people who can answer their questions. Do not make assumptions or unrealistic promises. The bottom line: Be sincere and be helpful.

Communication

The importance of timely and accurate communication with various entities cannot be emphasized enough in responding to a crisis. Communication begins with the flow of information from emergency response personnel (police, fire, EMTs, hospitals, etc.) to the crisis response team. On many campuses, the university police dispatcher is the central contact to activate the crisis team. Why? First, the university police have established contacts with community emergency response agencies. Second, these agencies are more likely to contact the university police and share important information about a crisis than they are to contact a university administrator. Third, the university police are informed of incidents that occur on campus. Fourth, the university police can help determine whether the incident requires the activation of the crisis team. Dispatchers and police leaders should receive training on the role of the crisis team. It has been my experience that the university police welcome the assistance of the crisis team and are quite willing to serve in the contact role.

The media relations office is another vital part of the communications plan. As soon as the crisis team has a clear understanding of the incident, it should contact media relations. As the official voice of the university, media relations should receive frequent updates on the incident. Media relations should be fully informed about all aspects of the crisis response; they should be very familiar with the crisis response plan and the role of the crisis team. It is important to clarify what information can be shared to help media relations understand the incident. It is the job of media relations to put the best face on what may be a negative incident for the university.

Each institution must determine the method of communication among university officials in a crisis. For a student affairs crisis team, the vice president for student affairs is typically responsible for informing the president and other vice presidents. I believe that the vice president should be informed once a crisis team member has evaluated the incident and has a clear understanding of what happened and which students are involved. The vice president should then receive regular updates. Depending on the magnitude of an incident, the president may inform the members of the board of trustees/regents. It may be important to share information with the university community as well—these communications may take the form of a mass e-mail, radio/television announcements, or an emergency telephone message. The director of media relations should be involved in drafting any message to the campus or the general public about a crisis.

Advances in technology have made communication among crisis team members easier. Before cell phones and pagers became popular, crisis response teams were activated via "telephone trees" and duty schedules with home and office numbers. Ideally, the crisis response team should always have a designated person on call, and that person should carry a pager. Using one pager gives the police dispatcher just one number to call, eliminating concern about who is on duty and how to contact that person.

In most cases, cell phones are an invaluable resource for the crisis response team. Obviously, they allow instant communications between members of the team and the police dispatcher, the vice president, and others. However, in a large incident or a weather-related incident, cell phones may not work. Too many cell phones in a contained area will overload the cellular grid and cause it to shut down, and weather can affect cell phone transmission.

We learned from the bonfire tragedy that some media satellite trucks have the capability of monitoring cell phone traffic. We were communicating sensitive information from the incident site to a crisis response command post in the office of the vice president for student affairs, and we couldn't figure out how the media were able to release this information within minutes of our cell phone communications. Only later did we learn that they were monitoring our conversations. Some institutions have purchased encrypted radios for communication among campus entities responding to a crisis.

Another issue with cell phones is that virtually every student has one, so information spreads rapidly in the student community. Controlling the accuracy of that information is difficult when hundreds of students are reporting to their friends and family about an incident.

Responding to an incident creates what I call the "spider web effect." At the center of the web is the incident and the student directly involved. From this center, connections radiate out to individuals and groups at various levels. Closest to the center are the people closest to the affected student: parents, siblings, roommates, and significant others. At the next level are friends, work associates, residents of the residence hall floor, and members of student organizations in which the student is/was involved. Farther away from the center are acquaintances, students enrolled in classes the student is/was taking, professors and advisors, the student's employer, and others who know/knew the student. Even farther out are individuals who have a need to know the information but may not know/have known the student, such as the registrar, director of financial aid, director of student counseling, director of media relations, and student newspaper editor.

What makes this scenario a web is the interactions among individuals at various levels and the fact that some students, faculty, and staff may know/have known a student in different ways. For example, a professor may have the student in a class, be the advisor to a student organization in which the student is an officer, and attend the same place of worship as the student. That professor will have a very different relationship with the student in this example than if the professor's only interaction with the student was in a management class of 400.

Parents of students affected by a crisis are a vital part of the crisis response. The crisis team is the conduit for official information to and from the university. As stated earlier, in the case of a student death, the police or coroner should make the initial contact with parents. The crisis team should provide support for the parents of affected students and keep them informed of what the university is doing and will do in response to the incident. These actions may include notifying professors, roommates, and student organizations in which the student is/was involved. They may include helping the students and their families make decisions about withdrawing from classes or making arrangements to box up a student's belongings. Sometimes, the crisis team's job is just to demonstrate the university's concern for the welfare of its students.

It can be very uncomfortable to sit with the family of a student in a hospital emergency room while they wait to speak with the treating doctor. It is much more difficult when the student is near death or deceased. I have learned that you don't need to speak; just being there is important to parents. When the doctor enters the room, I always offer to leave so the family can meet in private with the doctor. In almost every case, the family has asked me to stay. I have wept with parents over heartbreaking news. I have prayed with them when they or a hospital chaplain offered prayer. And I have helped them with sad tasks: contacting other family and close friends, considering the donation of organs, and contacting a funeral home. At these times, I try to simply be there for the family and support them in any way I can.

A parent or alumni association can be a very valuable resource in the response to a crisis. The Federation of Texas A&M University Mothers' Clubs was an invaluable resource to the CIRT. We found that the group (commonly known as Aggie Moms) was a valuable partner in assisting families. Because there are more than 125 chapters in Texas and beyond, there was usually a chapter close to the home of any student. In times of crisis, the Aggie Moms would call on families of involved students. Their support took many forms, from phone calls of support or condolence to families of students, to delivering covered dishes, to visiting students in local hospitals, to establishing scholarships in honor of deceased students. We also used the clubs to respond to critical incidents involving students that occurred away from campus; for example, an auto accident involving a student traveling home for the weekend or semester break. The Aggie Moms expressed interest in assisting when we first asked, but it was the CIRT's response to incidents involving the children of federation officers that took the group's involvement to higher levels. Many campuses have parent or alumni organizations that can assist in similar ways.

Relationship with Academic Affairs

A good working relationship with academic affairs is critical to helping students with academic issues related to a crisis. At large universities, each college may have an associate dean for undergraduate and graduate affairs; these are key individuals for working through the details of an interrupted degree plan or a student death. This function also can be performed by the registrar or other academic administrators who have the authority to make course changes beyond regular deadlines. Although students should always be referred to their academic advisor and individual faculty members; the associate dean's involvement can help with those referrals. A working relationship and regular contact between the crisis response team and the deans and departments make it easier for them to become involved and provide assistance to students in a crisis. This benefits the student, for obvious reasons, and benefits the school and the crisis response team as well.

On one occasion, a student who was participating in a boxing tournament struck a blow that eventually caused his opponent to die. Although he was extremely traumatized, the student wanted to try to stay in school; his family supported his decision, as long as he received personal counseling. As a safety net (with the student's permission), I contacted his associate dean to apprise her of the situation. The dean assured me that the college would do whatever was needed, regardless of the semester calendar. Her main concern was that the student was being cared for and receiving the assistance he needed. Once that was established, I simply provided the associate dean with an update at the end of the semester.

The office of the registrar is vitally important for withdrawing students and approving a variety of recorded and unrecorded drops from the university, and the admissions office has provided excellent guidance on the complicated readmission processes. Both the admissions office and the registrar recognized the involvement of the CIRT and made an effort to streamline processes. A letter of support for re-admission, written by the staff member who worked with the student, was all the documentation the admissions office required to explain a student's departure and interest in returning to complete his or her degree.

The value of these relationships was apparent in the case of a student who died a month before he was scheduled to receive a degree in mechanical engineering (ME). The student's grandfather, father, and older brother all had ME degrees from the university. Although a posthumous degree was certainly feasible, the family felt strongly about an earned degree. We contacted the ME department and learned that the student lacked just one course, which he was taking over the summer through correspondence from another university. We contacted that university and learned that he lacked only the final exam. Our ME department explained the situation to the engineering professor at the other school, who agreed to waive the final and award a grade. The registrars at both universities streamlined the transcript process and, within a day, I was able to deliver to the family the diploma for an earned ME degree. The framed diploma was displayed at the student's funeral. None of this would have been possible had I not developed working relationships with the associate dean in engineering and with the registrar. Everyone involved was proud that we were able to provide the student's family with a bit of comfort.

Managing Grief

A crisis responder deals with students and their families who have experienced a loss, whether it is an apartment damaged by fire, a serious injury, or the death of a loved one, close friend, or roommate. Dealing with loss is a difficult experience for everyone. Serious illness, an accident, loss of a loved one, or other trauma result in a mixture of feelings. "These feelings include sadness, fear, despair, confusion, anger, guilt, and even a sense of numbness. These emotions may be felt in varying degrees of intensity and over differing periods of time" (*Coping with Loss*, 2005). Members of the crisis team must understand that people grieve in their own ways and in their own time.

The first response to a loss is usually denial, shock, or numbness (*Loss and Grief*, 2005). It is important to allow students some time after an incident to get past the initial shock before discussing the grieving process, but students who may be experiencing loss and grief should be directed to the campus counseling service for assistance. We have found that students who were close to a deceased student often benefit from a "grief process session" held 24–36 hours after the incident. Counseling staff meet with groups of students and process what each person is feeling in response to the incident. Such sessions may be held in the residence hall where the student lived, at a meeting of an organization in which the student was involved, and/or in classes in which the student was enrolled. The grieving process may take as long as a year, so crisis team members should make an effort to maintain regular contact with students who were especially affected by the incident.

As a crisis responder, you may wonder how you can be helpful to a student during a time of grief. The Counseling Center at the University of Florida makes the following suggestions for assisting students and families affected by a loss:

- Communicate your concern for the person. Initiate conversation, listen, and be willing to talk about the loss.

- Be available. Let the person know that you are available, if you are needed.

- Avoid making judgments about how people should be feeling as they grieve. People express their thoughts and emotions in a variety of ways, with different levels of intensity and frequency.

- Acknowledge the difficulties in seeking answers to questions about life and death.

- Affirm the appropriateness of the questions and encourage conversation.

- Remember the importance of anniversaries, celebrations, and activities in which the loved one used to participate. Be sensitive to the memories that special occasions and activities hold.

- Reaffirm the value in your relationships. Be mindful of the importance of various types of relationships: friend, classmate, family member, neighbor, colleague, partner, or intimate.

- Be sensitive to the cyclic nature of the grief process. Be patient. Remember that grief can come and go for no apparent reason. There is no fixed time by which the grieving process is to be over (*Coping with Loss*, 2005).

One final note on the grief process: The crisis responder is also affected by the incident, even if the responder did not know the student. I have found it helpful in bringing personal closure to attend the funeral of a deceased student, especially if I was involved in responding to the incident.

Critical Incident Stress Management

In the weeks following an incident, the response team reviews its actions during the crisis. The purpose of the review is continuous improvement; however, it may fail to address the emotions that crisis responders experience. During the initial response, responders often describe a sense of being on autopilot—the training and experience kick in, and you react to the incident. It is when you leave the incident scene or hospital and go home that the emotions surface: You are acutely aware of the fragility of life and feel a need to be with loved ones. Whenever I return home from a crisis that has involved serious injuries or death, I need to be close to my wife and children. Even if it is 3:00 a.m., I go into my children's bedrooms to make sure they're safe, and to hug them.

CIRT members can be secondary victims of crisis and trauma. Many emergency services agencies use Critical Incident Stress Management (CISM) to help responders deal with their emotional response to a crisis. "CISM is a comprehensive, systematic, and multicomponent approach for the reduction and control of harmful aspects of stress" (Mitchell & Everly, 1998, p 11). Its purpose is to "maintain health and productivity, prevent or mitigate traumatic stress effects, restore personnel to normal functions, speed recovery from stress, enhance the overall environment in which the person works or lives" (p. 14). CISM has seven core components (p. 9):

1. Pre-incident preparation (before the crisis)
    A. Set expectations
    B. Improve coping skills
    C. Stress management education
2. Demobilization (immediately following the crisis)
    A. Inform participants about posttraumatic stress
    B. Psychological decompression
    C. Stress management tactics
3. Defusing (within 12 hours of the incident)
    A. Symptom mitigation
    B. Possible closure
    C. Triage
4. Critical incident stress debriefing (1–7 days after the crisis)
    A. Facilitate psychological closure
    B. Symptom mitigation
    C. Triage
5. Individual intervention (anytime)
    A. Symptom mitigation
    B. Return to function, if possible
    C. Referral, if needed
6. Family CISM (anytime)
    A. Foster communications
    B. Symptom mitigation
    C. Closure, if possible
7. Follow-up referral (anytime)
    A. Assess mental status
    B. Access higher level of care

I recommend that CISM be incorporated into the response process. Not every response will require defusing or critical incident stress debriefing, but your team should be aware of CISM and be able to implement it when appropriate. Emergency response agencies and hospitals in your community probably use CISM and have trained personnel who may be willing to assist you.

Whether or not an institution formally adopts CISM as part of its crisis response process, it is very important to assess how individuals on the crisis team are dealing with the emotional response to an incident. A team member should be permitted to say, "I cannot participate in crisis response at this time." The individual should be encouraged to seek counseling. A team member who is having emotional difficulty but is not willing to take a break should be confronted. In some cases, it may be necessary to remove a person from the team until he or she has dealt with the symptoms and is emotionally ready to return to crisis response duties.

Conclusion

While many universities have formal plans that address the physical aspects of a crisis on campus, these plans may not address the effects of the crisis on people. It is in this realm that student affairs plays an important role. It is recommended that a crisis response team be established within student affairs to address the special needs of students and their families. The team can be structured in various ways; however, it is important to recruit team members who have the appropriate personality, character, and skills to respond to a crisis. To ensure its success, the team should develop positive working relationships with key agencies on and off campus.

Crisis response requires the ability to evaluate a situation carefully and determine the best course of action. It also requires a willingness to sin bravely—to do the right thing rather than focusing on institutional reputation or potential lawsuits. And crisis team members must not forget to look out for each other—crises can take an emotional and psychological toll on responders.

References

Bornstein, J., & Wilson, A. (2004, December 7). *Creating a crisis management plan: Using the all-hazards approach (Part I)*. NetResults. Retrieved December 10, 2004, from www.naspa.org/membership/mem/nr/article.cfm?id=1477.

Coping with loss. (2005). Retrieved May 19, 2005, from University of Florida, Counseling Center Web site: www.counsel.ufl.edu/selfHelp/copingWith Loss.asp.

Critical incident response team. (2005). Retrieved April 20, 2005, from Texas A&M University, Department of Student Life Web site: http://cirt.tamu.edu/cirtgoals.htm.

Critical incident response team training manual. (2003). Retrieved December 14, 2004, from Illinois State University, Division of Student Affairs Web site: www.studentaffairs.ilstu.edu/CIRT/index.shtml.

Loss and grief: Tips for coping and recovery. (2005). Retrieved May 20, 2005, from Texas A&M University, Student Counseling Service Web site: www.scs.tamu.edu/selfhelp/elibrary/infos-heets.asp#personal.

Mamarchev, H., Paterson, B., & Whipple, E. (2002, November). *Campus crisis: Navigating through difficult times*. Presentation at the NASPA IV-East Conference, Skokie, IL.

Mitchell, J. T., & Everly, G. S. (1998). *Critical incident stress management: The basic course workbook*. Ellicott City, MD: International Critical Incident Stress Foundation, Inc.
Reber, T. (1995). Fish Camp policies and procedures. Texas A&M University, Division of Student Affairs.

Trauma response team. (2005). Retrieved April 19, 2005, from University of Florida, Dean of Students Office Web site: www.dso.ufl.edu/TRT.

Chapter 3

Spirituality in Crisis Response

Kristin S. Harper and Dawn L. Williams

Unlike most authors who write about spirituality, we have not studied theology or spent time in a seminary, and we do not have degrees in philosophy or divinity. We are *practitioners*; that is, average people who practice spirituality in their own lives. In this chapter, we describe the experience of allowing a very personal aspect of our lives—our spirituality—to enter into our professional lives, specifically at times of crisis. We also discuss opportunities to acknowledge spirituality in the institutional response to crisis.

The word *spirituality* can have many different meanings. For our purposes, we will use the concept developed by the Higher Education Research Institute (2004-2005):

> Spirituality points to our interiors, our subjective life, as contrasted to the objective domain of material events and objects. Our spirituality is reflected in the values and ideals that we hold most dear, our sense of who we are and where we come from, our beliefs about why we are here—the meaning and purpose we see in our lives—and our connectedness to each other and to the world around us.

> Spirituality also captures those aspects of our experience that are not easy to define or talk about, such as inspiration, creativity, the mysterious, the sacred, and the mystical. Within this very broad perspective, we believe spirituality is a universal impulse and reality.

> Spirituality does not have to be tied to a religious affiliation or a set of beliefs, although for many it is practiced through an organized religion.

Those of us who respond to crises learn certain standard skills. Each of us also develops response techniques that are more personal. Responders who have an understanding of their own spirituality may find an additional gift or talent at times of crisis—an understanding of the meaning and purpose of their presence in the moment. Spirituality can be seen as a hidden treasure, a reassurance that one's ability to "do the right thing" is genuine and significant to one's own experience and that of others involved in the crisis.

How do we find this hidden treasure within ourselves, and how do we recognize and acknowledge it in others? For many people, spiritual development begins with the religious training they receive as children; many hold those beliefs, or related beliefs, throughout their lives. As adults they may affirm the fundamental beliefs of their family as their own, and may go on to study and understand more about those beliefs. For others, the introduction to spirituality is not based on religion and may come from outside their family of origin. It might be triggered by an incident, another individual, or a search for meaning in their lives.

Whether one begins the journey with a traditional religious focus or in some other way, it is a starting point for developing an understanding of personal spirituality. The journey includes personal reflection, attempting to understand one's place in the world, interaction with others, and, ultimately, testing one's beliefs in various situations. These tests allow us to hold on to the beliefs that feel true and further explore those that are questionable.

Spirituality can be seen in crisis situations in the reaction and response of those involved. Student groups and individual students and their families who have strong religious or faith-based practices may draw on those customs in a crisis, for comfort and as a way of coping. Public prayer in the emergency room of a hospital or at the scene of a campus incident is not an uncommon sight, and crisis responders are often invited to participate.

At Seton Hall University, a father and mother who were removing the belongings of their daughter who had died in a car accident stopped to talk to her distraught floormates. The parents shared their faith and their pain. They cautioned the students about taking life too fast. This encounter made a difference in the experience of both the parents and the students. The parents took time to make a connection.

Regardless of one's beliefs, being part of such a moment with students, families, and the university community can be important for everyone. It acknowledges the role of spirituality in the lives of those in crisis. A responder who is connected to his or her own spirituality can derive personal meaning from the event and use the opportunity to connect and be present with those involved, without having to share specific beliefs or faith practices.

Spirituality can enter crisis situations through the responder. An individual responder's understanding of his or her own spirituality can play a significant role in the interaction with those in crisis. It is important to note that spirituality does not need to be identified to benefit others. It can simply be felt as "comfort of presence," a sense that the responder can handle the situation and go wherever the person or the situation is going. The comfort of presence manifested through the responder's spirituality is not the same as strong counseling and interpersonal skills.

While these skills are essential to help persons in crisis, they are learned skills that are directed to the individual in crisis. The comfort of presence, on the other hand, resides in the responder. The effect of both may be a strong connection with the individual in crisis, but the source of the latter is more intimate. It is understanding one's place or purpose in the moment, rather than the ability to communicate concern, that allows the responder to be fully present and comfortable.

The effect of spirituality on crisis response need not be obvious; in fact, on the surface the response may not differ from one without a spiritual component. What may vary is the motive, the intensity, and the intimacy of the response. In an intimate moment with a parent standing vigil at the bedside of her critically injured son, a responder takes the mother's hand and holds fast for several minutes. Physically connecting to another human was, for this responder, who she was and the right thing to do.

Spirituality can provide healing, comfort, and serenity to the responder who may witness human pain and suffering, death, and destruction not typical in the experience of a college administrator. While those affected by the crisis may grieve a loss and suffer pain, the responder witnesses all this pain and participates in many other aspects of the crisis, such as body recovery, notification of families, and helping students sort through belongings left after a fire or flood. A spiritual foundation can contribute to a sense of meaning and purpose that can provide comfort and peace to the responder.

Spirituality might also serve as a foundation from which to build professional experience. Comfort in working with people in crisis and our awareness of these unique skills might draw us to this work and guide how we perform it. For many, spirituality is simply the strength to carry forward in the face of unspeakable tragedy.

The spirituality of the responder can have a strong impact on the response. At times, it may be difficult to decide what to do in a crisis situation, and crisis response team members must trust one another's ability to do what is right. An understanding of one's own spirituality can add another dimension as responders seek to determine what to do and what their place is in the crisis. Spirituality is a gift responders can offer, without sharing the source or details of their personal beliefs.

Understanding their own spirituality can contribute to the overall health of responders. Practicing meditation, participating in religious services, or seeking out a spiritual advisor are common methods of finding inner peace and health. Experience with these practices can provide a strong foundation when responders are faced with situations that are difficult to understand or explain. Thus, practicing one's connection with personal spirituality should not be a response to a crisis situation but, rather, a way to strengthen one's ability to respond and to cope. A crisis team member had returned from a long-planned spiritual retreat just days before a residence hall fire that took the lives of three students. She believes that her attention to her spiritual development just before the incident gave her the strength to better respond to the crisis and be more fully present to her university community.

In crisis response, spirituality can provide a sense of wholeness to those responding to the crisis and to the victims. Spirituality allows the experience of humanness, a connection between people. It can be a path between who we are and what we do; it allows us to make our work personal without actually revealing our personal beliefs.

In a particularly devastating accident that involved the deaths of five visiting college students, a crisis response team member found herself describing to the mother of one of the deceased students her daughter's last few moments of life. The mother had read all the police reports, spoken with the responding officers, and even driven hundreds of miles to view the scene of the accident. The team member had written the reports pertinent to her own campus, but she had additional notes about a conversation with two students who had administered CPR to the dying woman. She was able to tell the mother that her daughter was not alone when she died; that two students were with her. One of the students, not knowing her daughter's name but wanting to provide comfort, held the young woman and called her "Baby." The responder had this information because she was present with the students at the scene and had made herself available later when the students needed to talk to someone about what they had seen and done. She was able to provide comfort to the grieving mother by telling her that her daughter had been held and soothed in the last moments of her life. This is not a typical aspect of crisis response; rather, it is the ability to be fully human and present in the face of tragedy and pain. Spirituality provides a foundation for this humanness, from which one can reach out to others.

Spirituality is a natural part of crisis response at private religious or church-affiliated institutions. The nature of religion is to provide answers when we can't make sense out of life, and certainly a campus crisis is one of those times. Schools with a religious affiliation rely on common faith beliefs and practices among their students and faculty as a source of strength and community. Public expressions of faith and belief in a higher power can be an important point of healing for an institution with such ties.

At a public institution or a private institution without a religious affiliation or history, faith beliefs and religious practices might not be part of the institutional response to a crisis. However, there are ways to acknowledge the spiritual and human experience without imposing a particular set of beliefs. A community gathering may include periods of silence during which individuals can engage in their personal practices. Designating a location for group or personal meditation, whether permanent or temporary, can help people heal, and spirituality can make its way into crisis response at nonsectarian institutions through the work of individual responders.

Chaplains are often part of crisis response teams at religious-affiliated institutions, but they may also be part of the response at public institutions, as an acknowledgement of the spiritual dimension of student lives. At Texas A&M, members of the Campus Ministry Association (CMA—an interdenominational group of chaplains and lay leaders that has a liaison relationship with the university) are regularly called on by responders to assist in critical incident response. In fact, CMA contact information is included in the Critical Incident Response Team manual. When students or families in crisis desire the participation of a leader of their faith community, the responder can quickly call a priest, minister, rabbi, or a Muslim Imaam. Although Texas A&M is a public institution, crisis response staff call on the CMA when they are responding to crises that affect the entire campus community. At those times, student counseling service staff members team with CMA members to provide comfort and support to students and to the entire community. CMA members respond as spiritual leaders, without particular reference to the traditions and beliefs of their individual faith communities. This relationship and common understanding of the role of spirituality has strengthened the institution's response to crisis.

The involvement of formal religious organizations is not the only way for spirituality to enter crisis response. Memorial services and prayer vigils are regularly held on college campuses during times of local or national tragedy, to honor seriously ill or injured students, or to memorialize students who have died. Student affairs staff and other administrators often play a key role in helping students organize these events, even to the point of making comments and offering common prayer during the event. Public affirmation of the power of spiritual beliefs as a means of comfort is highly appropriate at these times. After a residence hall fire in which three students died, Seton Hall University began each day with a community meeting that started and ended with prayer. These meetings were held the day of the fire and for a few days beyond the fire, as the crisis began to unfold. This changed the tone of the meetings from anger and hostility to solace and communal support.

Many of us at private and public institutions participated in prayer vigils on September 11, 2001, as a way of coming together to address our common fear and sadness, and to acknowledge the role of spirituality in coping with events that were unexplainable and beyond individual control. At many campuses, these vigils continued throughout the fall, bringing in more diverse groups and moving from prayers and meditations seeking comfort to those seeking peace.

Texas A&M has a unique tradition for memorializing deceased students. The program, Silver Taps, is held the first Tuesday of each month to honor Texas A&M students who have died during the previous month. On that day, the names of the students being honored are posted at the bottom of the flagpole in the central plaza. At 10:30 p.m. the campus lights are dimmed; to the sound of the carillon, hundreds of students quietly enter the plaza for a 30-minute ceremony to honor their fellow students. The ceremony is silent except for a 21-gun salute by the honor guard and the sound of three buglers playing a special rendition of taps called "Silver Taps." Students leave the ceremony in silence. In all, they spend about 60 minutes in quiet reflection, some alone, many with friends. Some students hold rosaries and other types of prayer beads; some use dim lights to read from books of mediation or prayer. Most students stand in quiet reflection; sometimes holding one another, surrounded by hundreds of others who are there to honor students whom they probably did not know. This public affirmation of the importance of memorializing the deceased makes a place for spirituality, opens the door for spiritual development, and acknowledges the spiritual beliefs of every student.

Perhaps the strongest place for spirituality in crisis response is in the need for closure for the students, families, and campus community, and for the responder as well. Memorial and prayer services and silent meditations to honor those affected by a crisis give us a place to come together. This time of reflection can strengthen the connections among those who were affected by the crisis, those who responded, and those who care about it. A memorial or prayer service on campus in honor of their lost student provides families with a way to connect with the campus community and have the comfort of knowing that their student is still considered a part of that community. This can be an important aspect of closure for families. The responder can look to these services, memorials, and funerals as a time of reflection and a time to connect with others in grief.

Spirituality is rarely mentioned in crisis management training, but for individuals and institutions, it can provide a foundation of strength on which to base the actions the responders and the institution will take. Acknowledging that there is a place for spirituality in crisis response, encouraging responders to explore the topic for themselves and their institutions, and recognizing the presence of spirituality in individuals and in the university community can add a new dimension to crisis response in higher education.

Note: The authors are grateful for the contributions of Reverend Robert Sterling Meyer, J.D., associate vice president for student affairs, Seton Hall University.

Reference

Higher Education Research Institute. (2004-2005). *Spirituality in Higher Education.* The spiritual life of college students: A national study of college students' search for meaning and purpose. Retrieved June 10, 2005 from University of California, Los Angeles, Graduate School of Education & Information Studies Web site: http://www.spirituality.ucla.edu/faq.html

Chapter 4

Balancing Responsibilities and Feelings

Editor's note: When we review our response to critical incidents, we typically look at the success of the response from the institution's perspective. Did we cover all the components of the plan? Did all responders do what they were supposed to do? Were there any procedural glitches? This chapter explores the people behind the incidents: the parents of a deceased student, a responder, the partner of a responder, a response supervisor, and a vice president of student affairs.

The chapter reveals very personal perspectives on crisis and crisis response. Some of the information in this chapter might seem too private to share. However, as the book developed, it seemed important to include these perspectives to provide a glimpse into the heart of crisis response work.

Each section of the chapter is written as a personal reflection; the sections written by professional responders include comments on how they have balanced job responsibilities with personal feelings.

Voice of the Parents

Dennis and Cathie Klockentager

The Klockentagers' son Mark was a student at Texas A&M when he died in 1999.

It is a privilege for us to participate in this collaborative effort. If we help just one family, it has been a worthwhile endeavor. We feel blessed to have a forum like this to talk about our son. There are two universal truths about parents who have lost children. Number one, parents love to talk about their children who have died. As long as they're remembered, they're not really gone. Number two, parents who have lost children don't ever "get over it"—the lucky ones just learn to cope with their new reality and carve out a new life. As two people who have spent time working with parents who have lost children, we can say that the ones who seem to "survive" the tragedy are those who have no regrets about the relationship with their child and have a sense of spirituality.

Our son Mark was born in Saratoga Springs, New York; died in College Station, Texas; and is buried in Urbandale, Iowa. He was born in upstate New York while we were serving on active duty with the U.S. Navy. He was the second of our two children, four years younger than his sister. He had a pretty normal childhood. He loved playing sports but discovered somewhere along the way that athletic talent was not his gift. Nonetheless, he never quit trying and always gave his utmost in all his athletic endeavors. His high school track coach even awarded him a letter despite his obvious lack of talent. The coach said that Mark may not have won a single race, but he had more heart than any young man he'd ever had the privilege to coach.

Mark was baptized Catholic, grew up attending mass regularly, completed his first communion, and was confirmed in his junior year of high school. In his senior year, he was a peer minister. After his death, the church named its annual male youth ministry scholarship in his honor. During the first presentation of the scholarship, the youth director noted that Mark's group may not have learned the most, but they had the most fun. Mark had a terrific sense of humor. He used it like a bridge, to connect with people easily and, more often than not, in very meaningful ways. Mark was also an outstanding student. It didn't always come easy for him, but he was willing to put in the time to achieve the results he demanded of himself. He graduated in the top 5 percent of his high school class.

From the time he was 10 years old, we lived in Lake Jackson, Texas. It's a very family-friendly community. He had great friends; in fact, through him, we were able to meet and make great friends as well. He loved life and seemed to have his priorities straight. He was the kind of kid you didn't mind investing time and money in. You just knew he was destined to succeed at whatever he decided to do.

Nothing could have prepared us for what ultimately happened. Mark died September 10, 1999, of a self-inflicted gunshot wound. He died of suicide. He left no note.

We usually talked with Mark every other day or so. Our conversations were not always long ones, but we felt in touch, connected, and in tune with what was happening in his life while he was attending college. We always looked forward to his calls. Given his schedule, it was easier for him to call us than for us to try to catch up with him. The night of his death, he had called to talk about his new job with the university. He was proud and excited; he had taken a job with the Alumni Association, soliciting contributions from former students. He said, "Dad, I just got the perfect job! For years, I've been asking you for money, and now I'm so good at it that I'm going to get paid to ask people for money." We had a great conversation that night. Thankfully, the last words we exchanged with him were "I love you." We had no hint of what was to come just six hours later.

Two weeks before his death—a year before his graduation from Texas A&M—Mark sent out law school applications. After his death, we purposely did not notify the Law School Admissions Council. Selfishly, we wanted to know if his dream of attending law school would have been realized. When we received an acceptance letter from the South Texas College of Law, we promptly responded, informing them of his death. Their return letter was signed by the president, who is also the dean of the College of Law. In the acceptance letter he said, "Our evaluation process is rigorous, detailed, and comprehensive. Applications and related materials are reviewed by Admissions Office professionals and the Faculty Admissions Committee. Please know that at each step of the process, Mark's application set him apart from his contemporaries. In fact, he was among the first of the class to be selected." Mark graduated from Texas A&M posthumously on December 15, 2000.

After we were notified of Mark's death, we headed up to College Station to claim his body. We first met with the College Station police, who informed us that we would not be able to see him until the next day at the funeral home. That night was the longest, toughest, and most unforgettable of our lives. We have never before or since felt so alone. We were totally overwhelmed by the circumstances, with seemingly no outlet for relief. The next day at the funeral home, we were met by one of Mark's best friends and his family. They had had the foresight to contact Student Life, so a representative of Texas A&M was also present. Looking back through the filters of time and distance, we can see that the mere presence of the Student Life representative set the tone for everything else that followed. From that point on, our load became lighter, and we began to see glimpses of daylight outside our shroud of darkness.

We assumed that Mark's death, which was front-page news in the school paper, would be perceived as a negative statistic and a liability to the image of the university, and that the university would act very "clinically" to quickly, quietly, cleanly, and unemotionally tie up any loose ends and distance itself from the tragedy and any stigma associated with it. We felt that Texas A&M had no real moral obligation beyond handling the business portions of the relationship; that is, to disenroll him, notify professors, and handle refunds for tuition and room and board. Much to our surprise and relief, that is not what happened. In fact, the university has treated us with great humanity from that very first meeting at the funeral home until this very day. Texas A&M fostered a very real sense of community and shared responsibility for our tragedy and our outcome. That Student Life representative who met us at the funeral home became our point of contact for any questions we had; and, believe me, parents who have lost a child have many questions. The representative "walked the walk" with us through everything that followed. We cannot emphasize enough how important it was to have one person—one *caring* person—through whom we could funnel all our requests and questions. We always received honest, accurate, and timely responses. An answer was quickly forthcoming for any question that couldn't be dealt with immediately.

Our experience with the College Station police was equally positive. The detective we initially met with was our point of contact for the legal side of this tragedy. He was professional, courteous, and cordial, and even gave us his pager number so we could reach him anytime, night or day, with questions. Different entities but the same response profile: a single caring point of contact. In responding to our needs, the university and the community functioned in tandem, not separately, which is no small achievement in today's complex world.

After Mark's death, the university offered us multiple opportunities for celebrating his life. These activities/traditions served as a springboard to help our family and the community as a whole begin to deal constructively with the tragedy. The activities served as both public expressions of shared grief and opportunities to begin moving from grieving toward healing. The activities were offered in a compassionate manner, and they were genuine, substantive, robust expressions of sympathy, not insincere gestures. These outpourings of caring and love helped to stimulate the healing process and created beautiful, indelible memories that will last a lifetime. We believe that those gatherings were crucial in setting the tone and pointing everyone affected by the death in the right direction, from tragedy to triumph.

In addition to the activities, we have vivid memories and keepsakes from other heartfelt university and community expressions that were served up to us and greatly enhanced our sense of belonging and being part of a larger "family." It is now obvious to us that the university is not an entity unto itself. The whole College Station community acted in unison to help lift, console, and support us. The lasting impressions we carry with us concerning this tragedy include these:

- Receipt of multiple bouquets of flowers from Texas A&M at Mark's funeral, flowers from different organizations at the university.

- Receipt of flowers from the management of his apartment complex. We never received a bill for cleaning his apartment after the tragedy occurred. The apartment management also allowed Mark's roommate to move to a different complex at no cost.

- A memorial service held by the campus ministry for Mark.

- A library book dedicated to Mark with a memorial inscription on the inside cover.

- A copy of The Aggie Network given to us by the Alumni Association.

- Silver Taps, a ceremony honoring students who have died while enrolled at Texas A&M.

- Muster, a ceremony honoring students and former students who have died.

- Posthumous graduation, where we walked in the graduation line, walked across the stage of Reed Arena, and received Mark's diploma from President Bowen, to a standing ovation.

On the basis of our experience, the blueprint for success in a campus tragedy dealing with a student should contain these elements, at a minimum:

- Always remember that you don't get a second chance to do it right—"it" being how the tragedy is dealt with from initial notification on.

- Inject yourselves early in a sincere and earnest manner. It is incumbent on the university to help frame the response. Early intervention and assistance is critical in deciding/determining the ultimate outcome from the parents' perspective. Their perception is the reality that the university will have to live with, right or wrong.

- Provide a readily available, sympathetic, and caring single point of contact for ALL questions from the bereaved, and leave no question unanswered.

- Provide heartfelt and genuine opportunities for grieving, both private and public, to all of those who are affected by the death. Let the parents dictate the responses to university and community offerings of support. Don't coerce participation.

- Be compassionate and caring, and don't worry too much about being politically correct.

- In striking a balance between institutional legalities and spiritual nurturing, err on the side of nurturing.

Practically speaking, there are some added benefits to be derived for the university if it meets or exceeds the expectations of a grieving family. These opportunities present themselves in the form of remembrance and celebration avenues.

- Since our experience with the university related to Mark's death, we have become outspoken ambassadors for Texas A&M.

- Most parents welcome the opportunity to immortalize their children after death, and the university provided gifting opportunities to enable us to do that: We have established a scholarship in Mark's name in the Mays School of Business.

- Parents do not want to lose their connection with anyone or anything that contributed positively in the aftermath of their tragedy. We have set aside a portion of our estate for Texas A&M, so that Mark will be remembered forever and we, as well, will be eternally linked to the university.

Finally, it should be understood that each death and each impacted family is unique. No two circumstances or responses will be the same. So many variables are at play that the only certainty in the family response is uncertainty. Dealing with parents who have lost a child requires a unique individual, an individual endowed with a servant's heart. To be granted that servant's heart is a gift. To recognize and embrace that gift is a blessing. To share that blessing for the benefit of others is a calling. To be faithful to that calling is a ministry. Each university has the opportunity to embrace that calling and provide that ministry, to indelibly touch many individuals, to affect forever many lives and help to heal untold numbers of families in crisis. To the world, each of those called to this ministry may be just one person; to the bereaved family, these people are the whole world.

University responders have the opportunity to be the catalyst, to help begin the metamorphous of bereaved families from grief to growth, from growing to glowing. We urge them to embrace the challenge.

Voice of the Responder

Kristin S. Harper

It took working through just a few critical incidents for me to realize that I would probably never use a response manual. A list of phone numbers and a packet of forms did come in handy, but nothing is as useful as a pad of paper and a pen. Responding to people in crisis—whether they are students, parents of students, family members, or colleagues—has always come naturally to me, so it is with some difficulty that I attempt to write about this professional experience.

The most important contribution from the university was the trust and support of my supervisor and the student affairs leadership. They supported the philosophy of "doing the right thing," which was my guidepost when making decisions on the fly. It was very important to know I would be supported even though my "right thing" might be different from that of another responder.

How do you ever know that you're doing the right thing? *Working Mother* magazine (2001/2002) used the term "sin bravely" in an article about work/life issues for women. When her company, which had had offices in the World Trade Center complex, needed to get back up and running after 9/11, Marilyn Carlson Nelson of Carlson Companies said, "We needed to get the facts, but then, as they say, 'sin bravely.' You just have to step forward and say, 'This is what we're going to do now, and we'll change it if new information comes in'" (p.40). For me, sinning bravely included always remembering and acting on the fact that I was Texas A&M University to many of the students and family members with whom I worked at a time of crisis. I was the personal side of TAMU, not the institutional side, and I believed that this gave me permission to respond personally and sometimes to take risks in order to do the right thing.

It was important to have respect for those involved in a crisis, regardless of their words, actions, or state of mind. I learned never to be surprised at how people reacted to a crisis. On various occasions I was included in very personal family decisions by people I had known for only a few hours; treated rudely by families, students, and emergency responders; and asked to help fully functional adults perform basic tasks, such as walking, writing, and dialing a phone. I did not believe that any of these behaviors reflected an individual's normal personality; rather, they were the result of individuals being placed in unusual situations. I think this perspective helped me avoid discomfort in meetings with students and their families.

Most students and families with whom I worked recognized that I had some experience with critical incidents and could offer them the benefits of this experience. One benefit was the relationships I had developed with hospital staff and local police and fire agencies, which allowed me access and information not usually provided to the public. For example, I was allowed in the emergency room with student victims; this afforded me the opportunity to provide information to friends of the student. Family members appreciated the simple things I could do, such as securing access for them to a private meeting room near the hospital emergency room or showing them the inside route from the emergency room to the surgery wing of a hospital to avoid contact with the media.

A fine line exists between respecting the privacy of students and families and knowing when and how to intrude. Sometimes I intruded for practical reasons: the ambulance had arrived to transport a student from one hospital to another, the hospital forms needed a signature, or a parent needed to take a critical phone call. On other occasions, I intruded for reasons of humanity. When I learned that a student in critical condition was not likely to make it through the night, I sought out his mother, who had traveled to town alone. We sat together in the hospital in total silence, occasionally holding hands. I knew when I decided to find the mother that she might want to be alone. If that had been the case, I would have left. But checking on her would still have been the right thing to do.

Because our response team had a good relationship with the local hospitals, hospital staff would regularly allow us in the emergency treatment room with an injured student. Fortunately, I have a stomach for blood, guts, and protruding bones! Emergency crews are not concerned about how much clothing they cut off; out of respect for the student, I always asked if he or she wanted to be covered and, if so, located a sheet. For some students, the idea that a university staff member saw them naked would be hard to get over. I made a point of standing where the student could easily see me and left the room when the student was being examined, unless I was asked to stay.

For many families, I was a resource person. I have tracked down police reports and medical specialists, personal items that a deceased student was carrying, and hotel rooms on graduation weekend when local hotels were fully booked. I have helped families and students process options related to academic, medical, and spiritual issues. Knowing when and how to refer is important in this role. A family or student in crisis isn't always willing to make another phone call or involve yet another person. For example, some families did not want to talk to the official at the morgue, so that was my role. Other families simply needed the phone number or location of the morgue. If the family or student had an obvious religious affiliation, I always offered to make a referral to a spiritual leader of their faith or belief. As a result of the CIRT's close relationship with the campus ministry association (CMA), we carried CMA members' home phone numbers, so we could call them for assistance and referral in response to critical incidents involving students.

I also had my own network. Sometimes I was too exhausted to complete all the tasks on my own. While responding to an apartment fire, I contacted a colleague and asked him to locate hotel rooms from the comfort of his home while I worked on identifying displaced students in a pouring rain that was clouded by smoke and cinder. Although I later gave him a hard time for getting the easy job, his assistance made a huge difference to me.

Probably the most critical skill needed to be effective in this work is the ability to establish boundaries. Although seeing people in extreme pain or sadness was difficult, most of the time I didn't know the injured or deceased persons and, therefore, did not share the pain and suffering. On one occasion, I did know the parent of an injured student. When the Texas A&M bonfire collapsed in the fall of 1999, killing 12 students and injuring at least 27, I was onsite immediately. It wasn't until late in the day that I recognized the name of one of the injured students, a young woman whose brother had been critically injured a few years before. I had worked closely with their mother at that time, and she and I later became friends. When I saw the student's name I realized that I would not have a clear boundary. I called my friend immediately and would have stepped in to "mother" her daughter until she could travel the eight hours to campus. Fortunately, her daughter was not seriously injured and she had already made arrangements.

Even with boundaries, it is easy to be drawn in to the extreme emotions exhibited in times of crisis and to become one of the victims instead of one of the helpers. Of course, I believe in being sympathetic, but not to the point of becoming enmeshed in the situation. It can be very easy to volunteer to do too much, to take over or take control. I think it's healthy to respond to the needs of people but not healthy to take over. I think appropriate response takes a mastery of skills, including listening, problem-solving, and respecting victims. And yet, having said that, I have been affected by some of the critical incidents I've responded to. I don't believe it was the incident itself that affected me but, rather, the interaction with the students and families, and what I learned from them.

An apartment fire killed one student and burned another. The emergency room staff contacted the parents of the burned student and told them that the student would be transferred by helicopter to the burn unit of a hospital in a major city near them as soon as the arrangements could be made. The doctors encouraged the parents not to make the two-hour drive to the hospital where their son was currently being treated, for fear he would already be in transit to the burn center by the time they arrived. Instead, the parents were encouraged to go directly to the receiving hospital (in the opposite direction) and wait for his arrival. The parents were frantic, and talking to them became my job. After relaying messages to and from their son, I began to describe everything I was seeing and hearing. I talked about what their son looked like and his state of mind. When I heard the helicopter approaching, I passed that information along and then described the landing, loading, and departure. At that point, we disconnected and they made the short drive to the receiving hospital.

A few years later, in a talk about critical incident response to a parents' club, I was describing this incident, along with a few others. After my speech, a woman I had never seen before walked to the front of the room and announced that she had come to this meeting just to give me a hug. She explained that she was the mother on the phone that night. Although we had spoken a few times after the incident, we had never met. She told the group that she had joined the parents' club because of the university's response to her family. I appreciated knowing how much my standing in a parking lot, looking up at the roof of the hospital, had meant to an anxious parent. A simple decision to do the right thing helped a student and his family and, in the long run, even affected the parent group.

The kindness shown to me by students and families in crisis has never ceased to amaze and humble me. I never expected that people would take time from their own very serious personal situations to write notes, send gifts, and publicly recognize my work. During one incident, I got up at the crack of dawn to travel via three airplanes to a small town in Texas to connect with the family of a student who had died. When the family of the deceased student changed their plans, they took the time to track me down at the airport to tell me they would not need my assistance, allowing me to return home instead of spending the day and night away from work and family. I will not forget their thoughtfulness. When I was pregnant with my first child, students and families with whom I had worked sent gifts for my baby. Every year at Christmas, I place on my Christmas tree a special ornament, a gift from the family of a student who died. Another family, whose son died of alcohol poisoning on his 21st birthday, allowed their experience to become public and, among other things, developed a 21st birthday card, complete with their talented son's artwork, that we send to every student during the month of his or her 21st birthday.

While strong, healthy boundaries were key to my responder skills, they were not always easy to maintain. Healthy boundaries require good emotional health, which for me meant maintaining good physical health with a healthy diet, regular exercise, and good sleep habits. I also counted on good friends, strong family support, and my personal spiritual beliefs to help maintain my emotional health. Having friendship and activity groups outside of work and away from work relationships was very important to me. The ability to refocus, put my work in perspective, and see the world moving on despite the tragedy of the day helped me stay balanced.

Just as knowing when to ask another responder to help is important, so is knowing when to ask for help in dealing with emotions and mental health. At our institution, the director of the Employee Assistance Program (EAP) was trained in Critical Incident Stress Management (CISM) and was familiar with our critical incident response program and the on-call team. Access to someone who knew the process, knew the people involved, and knew me was an incredible resource. On more than one occasion, I called or visited EAP to help me get back on track. Oddly, it wasn't the major incidents that challenged me; I think I was on such "high alert" during those times that I had everything, including my emotions, in check. Instead, it was the smaller incidents, where I might have overlooked something or had a questionable reaction or interaction, that troubled me most.

The impact of working with people in crisis is usually immediate. The physical impact often appeared as sleeplessness or the inability to concentrate. At work I would have to do more in less time and often be pulled in two different directions as I worked with students and families while maintaining my regular duties. This physical response to the stress of working with people in crisis usually passed in a few days or a week. The impact of this work on my life, however, has been long term. It was important for me to see past the pain, the fear, the sadness, and the grief I observed. Understanding and appreciating that somehow I might have provided direction, comfort, assistance, or a simple act of kindness that made a difference at that moment allowed me to maintain my physical and emotional health. I have chosen to accept this as a gift.

It may be obvious from previous paragraphs that I am a person with spiritual beliefs. My spirituality and faith practices were not something I offered to students and families but, rather, part of who I am. I didn't minister to students and families. I think there is a difference between connecting people with a priest, minister, or rabbi because I understand the value of faith traditions and ministering to them myself.

The opportunity to debrief after each and every response was a very important coping mechanism. Being able to process actions, and the thoughts and feelings that go along with them, helps the responder as well as those who listen and learn. Sometimes the debriefing from a minor incident netted the name of a helpful law enforcement officer or doctor; at other times, the debriefing simply allowed us to rehash the incident and put it into perspective. In one debriefing, I spoke of my regret over not accompanying a student affairs director to the out-of-town location of a student death at a university activity. I still regret that decision, but being able to discuss it with colleagues and the director helped me cope with what was probably a mistake in judgment.

During the time I had critical response duties, I went from being single to being married and having a child. At the beginning of my tenure, I did not have to balance my time with family; my immediate family lived in another state, and I used annual leave and weekends when I was not on call to visit family and friends. Other than feeding my cat, I was truly uncommitted. After I married I had to, for the first time, explain my whereabouts and share the middle-of-the-night pager rings. This took some adjusting, for both me and my husband. To be honest, he hated it; not because of the disruption but because of his concern for me. It took me some time to see things from his perspective; my first reaction was that on top of everything else when dealing with a crisis, I had to let him know where I was and how I was doing! We eventually came to an agreement on expectations for keeping in touch, but it was stressful for both of us.

Nothing else that I did professionally had such an effect on my home life. I understood the part of my work that took me away from a planned event or out of bed in the middle of the night, but my husband did not. I learned to review my on-call schedule with him before making it final and then mark the kitchen calendar with my on-call dates so he could see them. He learned that when I was up all night I would need time to recover and that sometimes I just needed to talk, even if it was the middle of the night.

Being pregnant on the job also proved to be a challenge, and managing the first trimester's fatigue while maintaining a full work schedule was difficult. Because my pregnancy was risky, my husband and I had decided not to disclose it until after the first trimester, so I couldn't always explain that I really was okay, even though I didn't look it. When it became obvious, students and families often were startled to see a pregnant woman as a responder ("No, I don't need to sit down"; "Yes, thank you—July"), but we worked through it. I did forgo a hospital visit with a student when his mother, out of concern for my pregnancy, called to tell me he had a contagious infection.

Having a child made things even more complicated. Not only did I have another person to worry about, but now I also had more things to juggle. I couldn't run to the hospital if I needed to pick up my daughter before the child care center closed. And with a small child at home, I didn't always have the option of taking an evening nap after a long night and day at work. After my daughter was born, the weeks I was not on call became more precious. I asked a lot of my husband, and I am humbled when I think of all he went through to support my work.

The work associated with my "regular job" didn't stop when a crisis occurred, so it was necessary to learn to balance regular duties with short-term, but often intense, projects. For many projects, deadlines were flexible and delays were possible; I relied a lot on the capable staff I supervised to adapt, adjust, and go with the flow when I was unavailable to them. They were adept at prioritizing and could identify the issues that needed to go to the dean in my absence. My colleagues in the Office of the Dean were also members of the on-call staff, so they were acutely aware of the importance of covering for one another. Having an assistant who could filter messages, find me wherever I was, and assign and reassign projects was also very helpful.

Unfortunately, not all deadlines are flexible, so there were times when I had to stay on track with a project while responding to an incident. It was those times when my family was most affected. Because I had some flexibility in my job, I could sometimes take time off later, once things calmed down, which allowed me to spend some extra time with my daughter. My husband, however, did not have flexibility in his job, so evenings and weekends really were our only time together. I learned to work smart during the day, packing in as much work as I could between 8:00 a.m. and 5:00 p.m. so my husband and I could have time together.

But sometimes being physically present when I was tired or distracted was barely worthwhile. I tried hard to separate work from home-life, but the physical wear and tear of work affected my time at home. My husband and I had planned a trip to the Grand Canyon over Thanksgiving in 1999. This turned out to be just a week after the tragic bonfire incident at Texas A&M. We had planned the trip for months and knew that our travel would soon be limited because of the arrival of our baby. It was important for us to go on the trip, but that meant I would have to let go of some responsibilities and separate from a very intense experience. The extreme change in scenery and the isolation of the Grand Canyon helped with that separation. Most important was the conscious decision to disconnect and immerse myself in the trip as a way of finding peace. On Thanksgiving Day, we decided to visit a nearby reservation rather than watching the Texas A&M vs. University of Texas football game (which was the inspiration for the bonfire tradition).

Serving as a member of the Critical Incident Response Team was an interesting and challenging professional experience. More important, it was an intensely personal developmental experience for me. It reinforced all I believe about human nature and professional and personal ethics. It enabled me to rely on my own unique set of skills, developed from personal and professional experiences and honed through work with other responders. In the end, I think I made a difference, and I find that to be extremely rewarding.

Reference

Finnigan, A. (2002). The Crisis, the Challenge. *Working Mother,* December 2001/January 2002, 27-40.

Voice of the Supervisor

Brent G. Paterson

According to Kevin Freiberg and Jackie Freiberg in *Nuts! Southwest Airlines' Crazy Recipe for Business and Personal Success* (1996), "[B]ehind most great companies there is a moral imperative, an obligation or sense of duty, that compels the company to operate in certain ways" (p.10). In developing the Critical Incident Response Team (CIRT) at Texas A&M University, and in our actions in responding to incidents, we had a sense of a moral imperative to assist students and their families during crisis.

In *Crisis Leadership*, Klann (2003) posits that, "Effective crisis leadership boils down to responding to the human needs, emotions, and behaviors caused by the crisis. Effective leaders respond to those emotional needs as those needs are perceived by those experiencing the crisis, not just to their personal perception of what those emotional needs are, might be, or should be" (p. 8–9). Klann has articulated the purpose for a student affairs crisis response team, a key role for the leader, and the importance of selecting the appropriate people to be members of the team. It is easy to impose your own beliefs, values, and expectations when responding to a crisis; however, the crisis responder must be able to adjust to the needs of the affected parties, and the supervisor must ensure that crisis responders meet those needs.

Klann identifies three essential characteristics for effective crisis leadership: communication, clarity of vision and values, and caring relationships. He says, "By paying attention to these themes, leaders can hope to increase their understanding of the human dimensions of a crisis" (p. 1). From the beginning, the CIRT clarified the vision and values that would guide the student affairs response to a crisis. We emphasized clear and frequent communications with those affected by the crisis and those who had a need to know. Above all, we provided a caring response at a time when others were focusing on the practical or legal aspects of the crisis.

As dean of student life at Texas A&M, I was the direct supervisor of the CIRT members in their university positions. I was also a CIRT member. At Illinois State University (ISU), I supervise some of the members of the CIRT in their university jobs and provide leadership for the CIRT. Rarely have I felt any conflict with these multiple roles. On both teams, we were able to develop confidence and trust in each other's abilities so we could operate as a team without being concerned about our titles or other roles. The trust came easy at Texas A&M, because the four of us had worked together daily even before the formation of the CIRT. Trust and confidence in each other's abilities have developed more slowly at ISU. There we were imposing a new system for handling crisis situations in an environment that did not see the need for such a system; we've had to overcome territoriality and the physical separation of team members, whose offices are spread across campus. Still, we have made tremendous strides in developing trust among the CIRT members, with the campus community, and with local emergency response agencies.

In the student affairs crisis response systems at both schools, the first responder from the CIRT becomes the person in charge of the student affairs response to the incident. Although I am nominally the team leader, my role in each incident is to assist the designated team leader for that incident. I believe that the members of the team develop as a group and as individuals because they do not rely on the supervisor to make decisions. This is especially critical when I am out of town or not available when an incident occurs.

Perhaps the most difficult part of being a supervisor and serving on the CIRT is the lack of control. I am not a person with a strong need to "be in charge," but there have been times when the vice president expected me to know more about a situation than I did or to be on the scene of an incident when I was not. Because I have confidence in the abilities of the other CIRT members, I do not immediately respond to an incident unless I receive a call for assistance from the CIRT on-call person. I learned to be comfortable saying to the vice president, "So-and-so is responding to the incident. I am confident that he/she has things under control and will contact me if he/she needs assistance. I assume so-and-so is keeping you informed." Over time, the team learned when I needed to be informed of an incident immediately (usually at 2:00 or 3:00 a.m. on a weekend) and when the call could wait until first thing in the morning. The crisis response systems we established at both schools were not hierarchical; rather, they involved the persons who were affected and those who needed to know.

I received a call very early one Sunday morning from the vice president, asking me about an accident outside a fraternity house in which three pedestrians were struck and killed by a student who fell asleep at the wheel. I had just returned a few hours earlier from an out-of-state meeting and knew nothing about the situation. The vice president implied that I should have been at the scene of the accident, directing the CIRT response. Groggily, I informed the vice president that I was confident that the CIRT person at the scene had things under control and would call me if I were needed. After I hung up, I considered getting dressed and going to the scene, but I decided that, in fact, I *did* have full confidence in the CIRT responder and the rest of the team. The next morning, I contacted the on-call person. She described the accident and the CIRT response, which was appropriate in every way. I share this incident to illustrate that even though I am the supervisor, I do not need to be involved in responding to all incidents.

There are always opportunities to offer ideas, suggest ways of addressing a situation, and assist in processing a response. I have tried to operate as a member of the team, not as a supervisor telling his staff what to do. On a few occasions, it was necessary for me to step into the supervisor role in responding to a crisis because the vice president had specific expectations. On such occasions, I always explained the situation to the other CIRT members. And I can honestly say that the vice president's expectations were never without merit.

Following each response to a critical incident, it is important to review what happened, what worked well, and what might be improved. These sessions provided a wonderful opportunity for learning and setting expectations for future performance. I expected the members of the CIRT to be as honest in their appraisal of my performance as I was in appraising theirs. Staff can be reluctant to provide honest feedback to a supervisor, but it was important that we evaluated each other's performance honestly, since we relied on each other in crisis response. I have a tough skin and did not hold it against anyone who provided honest feedback.

It is essential for the supervisor to constantly evaluate the emotional and mental state of crisis response team members. From the beginning, the members of the CIRT at Texas A&M recognized the need to look out for each other. We often discussed our fear of responding to an

60

incident to find that one of the victims was a student we knew inside or outside the classroom. Fortunately, such incidents were rare.

There are times when personal issues will necessitate a person removing him- or herself from the CIRT; in some circumstances, the supervisor may have to remove a person from the team. Someone who is dealing with a divorce, serious illness, death in the family, or other personal trauma will find the emotional stress of responding to a critical incident or crisis extremely difficult. The person's coping skills may be depleted to the extent that he or she cannot fulfill the CIRT role. We were a close-knit group, and I knew the spouses and children of the other CIRT members. At times, I would hear how an incident affected not only the CIRT member, but also his or her family. I place a high value on balance in one's life. When I thought a team member's life was getting out of balance, we would discuss what could be done. Sometimes the solution was as simple as my saying, "I don't want to see you in the office the next few days. Stay home, go visit family or friends, spend time with your children." In some cases, there are no simple answers for personal issues, and it takes a concerted effort over time to reach resolution.

As the supervisor, I tended to feel that I should show unwavering leadership and should not display any emotion. These feelings are exaggerated by the male psyche, which calls on men to show strength in time of trouble. I do not typically display a great deal of emotion, so others expected the calm exterior. Plus, I found that in the middle of a critical incident or crisis, there was no time to be emotional. And I was fortunate in never having a previous personal connection with the students or parents involved in an incident to which I responded. My reactions came later, in the next day or two, when I realized what had happened and how the lives of students and their loved ones had been affected.

Our team adopted the concept of Critical Incident Stress Management (CISM) (see chapter 2 for more information on CISM), and it became an integral component of our process. Along with other crisis responders at the university, we all completed the basic CISM course. The trainers noted that supervisors are usually pulled out of stress debriefings with staff, because staff are afraid that what they say may affect their jobs. At the same time, supervisors do not want to discuss any emotional difficulties they may be experiencing in front of their staffs.

The first time we used CISM was after the bonfire tragedy in November 1999, in which 12 students died and at least 27 were injured, some very seriously. The initial responder from the CIRT had been visiting with some of the students working on the bonfire only a few hours before the tragedy. She knew several of the students who died and were injured. Other CIRT members assisted the families of those who died and those in local hospitals. It was a week before we were able to have a special debriefing.

The debriefing was very difficult for me as a supervisor. I had a senior staff member who was traumatized by the incident. It was important for her to share her emotions and grief, and I had to make some administrative decisions about her continued role on the CIRT and her ability to perform her duties as a staff member. The other two CIRT members obviously had been affected by the crisis but seemed emotionally stable and able to perform their regular duties.

I also had to deal with my own guilt, which I still carry. I was out of town on a job interview at the time of the bonfire collapse. Staff tried to contact me immediately after the initial report but were unable to reach me. (The switchboard at the university conference center where I was staying was closed from midnight until 6:00 a.m.) After returning from an early morning jog, I received a phone call from a CIRT member. I listened as she described what had happened but was unable to comprehend the magnitude of the situation. When she finished, I asked, "Do you want me to come back?" This may seem like a ridiculous question, but I did not want to imply that they could not handle responding to a crisis on their own or that I needed to be there to take charge. She responded, "Yes, get back here as soon as you can." I caught the first available flight back to College Station.

I felt that I let my colleagues down by not being there to provide assistance and support. Rationally, I know that I returned to campus rested and was able to relieve others who had been responding to the needs of students and their families for 16 hours, but I still felt guilty. However, I did not share those feelings in the debriefing. I felt that I needed to be the pillar of strength for those who had been involved in the response from the beginning. I believed that I should deal with my feelings personally, not in front of others who had endured much more than I had.

Adding to my feelings of guilt was the fact that I had to be away from campus a few weeks later. We were still enmeshed in visiting students who remained in the hospitals, working with students who were at home recovering, and assisting the many students who were friends of the deceased and seriously injured. I had arranged months earlier to help my father move from Pennsylvania to Tennessee. This was a big move for him. He and my mother had lived in the same house for more than 40 years. My mother passed away 5 years earlier, and my brother and I had convinced him to move to Tennessee to live near my brother. I knew that the CIRT and staff would manage in my absence, but I hated to leave them again. (The deaths outside the fraternity house mentioned earlier had occurred that same semester.)

My absence when the bonfire collapsed created another emotional issue for me as a supervisor. Until then, whether I personally responded to an incident or not, I always felt connected and felt that I had played a role in the response. The bonfire crisis was different—I did not share the same experiences as other responders. Everyone else had responded immediately to the crisis and had dealt with many concerns before I returned to the campus. Because so much had already happened, I did not feel connected to the decision making regarding the ongoing response. I felt like an outsider and deferred decision making to others who had been involved from the beginning. I could not and cannot relate to the incident in the same way as those who were immediately involved in the response.

In the months that followed the bonfire crisis, one of the CIRT members decided that responding to calls was causing too much emotional stress and asked to leave the team. Of course, I granted her request and encouraged her to continue counseling to deal with the posttraumatic stress she was experiencing. At that time, we all loathed being on call, fearing that we would have to respond to another crisis, so we expanded the CIRT membership to include a few key staff members in student life and the office of the assistant to the vice president. Our close-knit team of four became a team of six, housed in three separate buildings. More than ever, communication, clarity of vision and values, and caring relationships were important leadership characteristics. Today, I face another challenge in providing leadership to the CIRT at ISU. My wife, who is the dean of students, is also a CIRT member. (I do not supervise her; we both report to the vice president for student affairs.) As a dual-career couple with two school-age children, balancing our professional and family lives can be challenging.

Should there be a major crisis at ISU, we will still need to care for our children. We will feel torn between our roles as crisis responders and parents. Fortunately, our older daughter (14 years old) is very responsible and capable of taking care of our younger daughter (7 years old) for a reasonable amount of time. We were tested recently when an off-campus apartment building burned to the ground. My wife and I were the initial responders to the fire, and we organized the CIRT response for the 90 students who were without their belongings or a place to live a few days before finals. While other team members were answering phone calls, developing a list of affected students, and identifying the students' needs, I picked up our younger daughter from the after-school program and took her home. Our older daughter made dinner, helped her sister with her homework, completed her own homework, and helped her sister get to bed. The exhausted parents arrived home later that night.

The Patersons are not unique in facing conflict in their roles as crisis responder, spouse, and parent. I have listened to student affairs colleagues in the Washington, D.C., and New York City areas discuss the personal conflicts they faced on September 11 in deciding how to respond to both campus needs and parental duties as their children were being released from school early. I have also listened to colleagues discuss the dilemmas they faced when hurricanes threatened their campuses and their homes. Somehow, we prioritize what needs to be done and survive in very difficult times.

Responding to a crisis can be one of the most difficult tasks we are asked to perform as student affairs administrators; yet, these situations can also be some of the most rewarding experiences of our careers. The rewards come from helping others cope under extreme circumstances and knowing that you have made a difference in their lives. I am always amazed when I encounter a student or family member months or even years after an incident, and they continue to express their appreciation for the CIRT response. I view the response as part of our work. They see it as much more.

References

Freiberg, K. L., & Freiberg, J. A. (1996). *Nuts! Southwest Airlines' crazy recipe for business and personnel success.* Austin, TX: Bard Press.

Klann, G. (2003). *Crisis leadership: Using military lessons, organizational experiences, and the power of influence to lessen the impact of chaos on the people you lead.* Greensboro, NC: Center for Creative Leadership.

Voice of the Vice President

Arthur Sandeen

I write from the perspective of both dean of students and vice president for student affairs. In those two positions, there are very few crisis situations I did not encounter. Nevertheless, I express my thoughts here with caution, as I would never suggest that the way I responded to crises was either the right way or a prescription for others. Crisis responses are best understood in the context of time, institution, and community.

Whether an incident is a crisis can differ from campus to campus and from one person to another. In 1968, it was certainly a crisis when 1,500 students moved into the ROTC armory to disrupt classes. In the same year, it was also a crisis when a doctoral student in physics took his own life by shooting himself. Some university presidents considered it a crisis when students peacefully demonstrated against institutional policies in front of the administration building—so these demonstrations became a serious issue for the student affairs staff. When a group of minority students threatened to withdraw from school because of inadequate financial aid, this was a crisis. If 1,000 students were "streaking" though the campus at 2:00 a.m. and the police called the senior student affairs officer at home, this could be termed a crisis. When students were raped, assaulted, or murdered, this certainly was a crisis. If a terrible tornado or hurricane strikes the campus, surely this is a crisis. Just like most senior student affairs officers, I was intimately involved in all of these.

Here are five thoughts about crises that reflect my experience and personal views.

1. It is our job to handle crises, and handle them well.
In the past 30 years, the student affairs field has grown impressively; the growth has resulted in considerable fragmentation and guild-type behavior among some of its segments. This has made it much more difficult to create a unified purpose among the various departments in a large student affairs program and has resulted in some dangerous confusion among those outside of student affairs as to what its purpose might be. Indeed, some professionals in the field reject the notion that student affairs should even be involved in handling crises. They argue that the student affairs role is purely education or service, and that others (such as the police) should handle crises.

My view is that it is our job to handle crises, and handle them well. We should be the best prepared of anyone on the campus to do this, and our presidents, faculty, alumni, and governing boards expect us to do it. Student affairs leaders should be the most knowledgeable persons on their campuses about how to respond to crises, and they must assume this responsibility. Whether senior student affairs officers like it or not, they are often judged by the president, the faculty, and the community in direct relation to their ability to handle crises. Moreover, if student affairs professionals are passive and allow others to assume leadership in crisis situations, their overall role on the campus will be diminished. But most important, it is their professional responsibility to handle crises.

I experienced the same kind of anxiety and dread that most people have when they enter a crisis situation, and I had the same tendency to avoid doing unpleasant things, especially with students. Luckily, I understood my own strengths and weaknesses well enough to know what I was capable of doing in a crisis. No one can do it all. I knew I needed to maintain my personal control; get enough food and rest; get some exercise—in other words, I knew I had to stay healthy, both physically and emotionally. But I was never alone. We responded to crises as a team.

2. All student affairs staff can contribute to crisis management.
There are many needs in responding effectively to crises. Good student affairs leaders find ways for people to be helpful in a crisis. No one is equally good at counseling, speaking to an angry crowd, dealing with grieving parents, responding to irate community members, and negotiating with a group of protesters. But, in every student affairs staff, there are individuals who can do each of these things, and the quality of response will be greatly enhanced if those skills are identified and used. It is the responsibility of the senior student affairs officer to see that this happens. When staff members find ways to be helpful in a crisis, they grow professionally, and the staff's sense of community is enhanced. Positions and titles are usually quite unimportant in this situation; every person should be asked for ideas and invited to participate.

3. Written plans are important, but effective relationships are the key.
Written crisis plans are a very good idea, and most institutions now have them. If they have been written with wide participation and given ample visibility, the chances for successful response will be improved. But a written plan will not work if close and trusting relationships have not been maintained over time among crucial campus and community leaders. This is especially critical for senior student affairs leaders, who should know city managers, commissioners, police chiefs, community business leaders, clergy, and other off-campus personnel on a first-name basis. The worst possible time to meet such persons is during a crisis. The responsibility for creating these relationships lies with the senior student affairs officer.

It is just as important for the senior student affairs officer to earn the confidence and support of the president, the other vice presidents, and members of the governing board. If the senior student affairs officer has established him- or herself as the leader in such situations, these key people will find it natural that student affairs assumes this role. People become highly emotional during crisis situations; if student affairs leaders have established positive relationships with their many constituent groups, they will be in a much better position to respond to the inevitable anger, frustration, fear, and sorrow that will surface.

Establishing trusting relationships with others (faculty, administrators, police, community leaders, student leaders) is what we should do best in student affairs. We earn respect and establish trust by proving that we are competent, honest, reliable, and available.

4. No martyrs need apply.
Some people are more effective than others in responding to crises. Those who are good at it have developed these skills over many years. Senior student affairs officers should know their staff very well and know which staff members to involve and which ones to protect in any given situation. It is the leader's responsibility to see that the institution

responds in the most humane and sensitive way; to ensure that this happens, certain staff members may have to be asked to back away.

A staff member who is overly involved emotionally in a crisis or one who has a personal agenda regarding an issue is a liability to the institution and may cause real harm to those in need. At times, some staff members may try to carry too heavy a load in a crisis, demonstrating almost superhuman dedication and energy day after day and night after night. It is the responsibility of the senior student affairs officer to prevent this from happening. In addition to the possibility of personal burnout, overly zealous responders can be a source of great irritation to others working on the crisis, and to the institution as well.

5. An institution reveals its soul during a crisis.
Senior student affairs officers should know the culture of their campuses very well. They should understand the values and expectations of their governing boards and presidents, know the history of their institution and what it means to its alumni. An institution is what it is; it rarely, if ever, reveals itself to be something different during a crisis. Its "soul" is there, in place, and student affairs leaders should know and understand what this soul is and be comfortable with it.

Senior student affairs officers should also know that whether the crisis is a suicide, a destructive storm, or a disruptive building takeover, the world will be watching to see how the institution responds. In a crisis, does the institution revert to an authoritarian decision-making process or does it strive to maintain an open, democratic, participative approach? In a crisis, are individual rights trampled to maintain a public image of control, or are sometimes nasty and angry views considered honestly in open debate? In a crisis, will strictly legal considerations regarding a student death outweigh moral obligations to the family? In a crisis, will the institution be seen as acting in its own interest or in a way that respects the victim? A crisis always reveals what an institution's values are, and the senior student affairs officer is the point person in ensuring that the response accurately reflects those values. He or she cannot change the values and soul of the institution but can act in humane, sensitive, and thoughtful ways. Responders should never forget that in the public responses they make in a crisis situation, they are "teaching," as others watch and evaluate how and what they do. If a senior student affairs officer experiences serious conflict between his or her own values and those of the institution, it is time to seek new employment.

When it came to determining what was the morally right thing to do, I was lucky: I spent many years, especially as an undergraduate, studying philosophy, religion, and psychology, almost entirely with the goal of trying to figure out myself and my life. Thus, by the time I was dean of students at age 28, I had, for the most part, worked out what the "right thing" to do was. If I had not known myself and had firm beliefs about students and higher education, I cannot imagine how I might have functioned, especially during the turbulent years of 1967–1973.

At almost any institution, there are times and events that cause us to question whether we can continue working there. It may be a president who speaks to the public about some issue in a way the student affairs officer knows to be completely untrue; it may be too many exceptions made to the stated admissions policy in favor of the children of wealthy alumni; or it may be a "conscience" issue for the student affairs professional about his or her "fit" with the student population. For example, I was offered the dean's position at Princeton in the late 1970s, but I knew that I was not a good match for those students; my place was with less advantaged students in public schools.

I was extremely lucky in my career to be able to do things I passionately believe in, working in institutions I viewed as mostly humane and supporting. By far the most rewarding experiences involved direct contact with students—getting to know them, watching their growth (or lack of it!), and seeing their successes in life after college. I worked very hard to maintain a lot of personal contact with a lot of students, and my major regret is that I did not do even more of this. Student affairs work is "helping students succeed," and this is the best part of all.

Voice of the Responder's Partner

Cheri L. Zdziarski

It is 3:00 a.m. The shrill beeps of the pager pierce the darkness. The heart pounds, muscles tense, mind races, and adrenaline surges as the body braces for the unknown. What critical incident or tragedy has affected a student or group of students: sexual assault, auto accident, alcohol poisoning, apartment fire, life hanging in the balance, life lost? The possibilities race through the mind in a split second, although it seems like an eternity while the details are learned and action is being determined. Whether it is 3:00 a.m. or 3:00 p.m., the emotions are the same—a critical incident has occurred and students' lives could be in danger.

Although this is a description of the reactions of the responder, as the partner of a responder, I experience many of the same intense, adrenaline-spiked emotions and reactions to a middle-of-the-night crisis. Once past the jolt of an abrupt awakening, my primary emotional response is usually fear. Only the responder is privy to the details of a situation as it unfolds. Out of respect for the family's need to resume normal activities, he often leaves the room to make the call. However, this leaves the partner (and sometimes the child) alone with a jumble of thoughts and emotions and uncertainty.

It is difficult to discuss in a clear manner the emotional impact of being the partner of a responder. The experience includes a wide range of emotions—from extreme highs to extreme lows—and they sometimes seem to come all at once. They become so enmeshed with one another that it is hard to identify them individually, but the negative emotions are more prevalent and deserve discussion.

I'm awake, and falling asleep again won't be easy, because my mind is focused on the events that are unfolding. Sometimes I catch enough from the one-sided phone conversation to piece together a basic understanding of the nature of the situation. While I feel compassion for those involved, I also feel a great sense of inadequacy that I cannot be of more help to either my spouse or the students and families involved. As a student affairs professional myself for almost 25 years, I have a strong desire to be of substantive assistance, but I find that once I have ministered to our child's needs (my number one priority in a crisis), there is not much I can do other than be available to meet some immediate physical need: brew a pot of coffee, grab pen and paper, boot up the computer, or maybe give my husband a hug. Sitting on the sidelines is difficult. With only a general awareness of what may be happening, I begin to worry about the students' families. Is the situation serious enough that parents will have to be notified? Fear and concern for those involved make it difficult to return to a restful sleep. This lack of sleep, especially during the weeks when my husband is on call, often affects everyone in the family. Irritability is a natural by-product and, over the course of the week, any one of us might say, "I'm sorry if I'm cranky…I just need to get some sleep."

Our daughter also is affected. Seldom has she slept through an emergency phone call. When she was younger, we just had to provide reassurance and comfort to a child who had been startled out of a sound sleep. However, as she grew older and became more aware of the nature of these calls, she was less easily calmed and became more inquisitive. She, too, wanted to know what was happening, if anyone was hurt, if someone had died. And she needed assurance that her father was okay—that he was just responding to a situation where a student needed help.

A child in the home presents a complex challenge for both the responder and the partner. We had to decide how much information to disclose at a particular age level to alleviate her natural childhood curiosity and fear without creating a premature loss of innocence. The primary question always seemed to be how much of the situation we could share with her without simply creating more anxiety for her. The child of a responder may learn earlier than parents might wish that the world is not always a safe place and that bad things happen to young people. For our family, I believe it has been a fairly smooth transition from the early years, when it was easy and necessary to be extremely vague about the nature of a crisis, to the later years, when it became more challenging to help a maturing teenager understand that, although many crises are the result of an unavoidable accident or disaster, others are the direct result of poor choices made by individuals.

Ever the educators, we believe that crisis response has provided important teachable moments in our child's developmental process. If there can be a positive side to a critical incident or crisis, it might be that the situation helped others learn, for example, that drinking alcohol to excess, jogging alone at night in dimly lit areas, or attending a party where you know few, if any, of the other partygoers are unwise choices. Unfortunately, young people frequently make these kinds of choices, with little appreciation for their potentially devastating consequences. I believe that the careful explanations we've given in response to our teenager's natural curiosity and concern have helped her develop compassion for people in crisis, as well as knowledge that her own judgment is critically important, that she has the power to create or prevent a life-or-death situation. When she was asked how her father's role as a responder has affected her, she said that she thinks she is better able to handle difficult situations because she has seen how her parents respond to crisis.

I believe that in the initial stages of responding to a crisis, the responder needs to be free to work without distractions. That knowledge, however, doesn't prevent my emotional reactions. I still feel the occasional twinge of jealousy that my partner's attentions are focused elsewhere besides with our family. I sometimes get that "martyred" feeling when I have to arrange or rearrange family, work, and extracurricular schedules because he will not be available as planned to drop our daughter off at school, attend a school event, or be home for dinner. After all the years that crisis response has been part of our lives, and considering my pride in my husband's involvement and expertise, I am amazed that these feelings have not disappeared, and I feel a little ashamed of my momentary lapses into anger or frustration at a time when others are dealing with sometimes incredible heartbreak and loss.

It is this polarized nature of the emotional reactions that is most difficult to manage. Feelings of frustration and disappointment go hand in hand with feelings of pride and respect: frustration that dinner plans or help with a project have been interrupted or delayed; disappointment that my husband is unable to attend a special event at our daughter's school; pride that he has the skill to take charge, be effective, and provide stability; and respect for his ability to think and act quickly and maintain integrity.

Learning to separate the normal, everyday family and marital annoyances from those related to the responder's professional commitments can have a great impact on family harmony. Being caught up in the demands of a crisis situation and unable to communicate with family members is a very different situation than being caught up in work and forgetting to communicate a change in schedule. Discerning the nature of the situation before reacting to a lack of communication can curb an inappropriate emotional response that might exacerbate a situation that is already highly emotional on many fronts.

Amidst this confusing array of emotions, it is important to recognize that these reactions are normal and that we can learn to move beyond the negative emotional state to maintain personal and family health. Open and effective communication between the responder and the partner is crucial. Both must actively work to keep communication lines open in the family, so everyone knows it is okay to express disappointment, irritation, and frustration. Expressing these feelings in the most appropriate manner is not always easy, but it is critically important and creates one more challenge to both responder and partner. Body language and verbal exchanges are powerful tools for teaching other family members positive forms of emotional expression. I must admit, that, on occasion, my personal examples have been neither positive nor acceptable. But I believe that even these moments of unacceptable expressions of anger and aggravation, if openly discussed and processed in the family, can be the basis for teaching the value of an appropriate response. It goes back to the importance of open and effective communication, not just between responder and partner but among all family members. Children benefit just as much, if not more, from hearing an adult say "I'm sorry" to another adult as they do from having someone say "I'm sorry" to them. The willingness to sit down with a child and discuss what was appropriate and inappropriate about our own behavior makes it easier to discuss these same things when *their* behavior is involved.

The impact of a crisis on a responder's partner and family is often overlooked. Although it can be difficult for the partner and family to maintain any sense of normalcy during a crisis, it is important for the crisis responder to be able to focus on the incident and not be worried about a partner or family member during such situations.

Chapter 5

Crisis Response: Real-Life Examples

In this chapter, we asked student affairs colleagues to share memorable experiences in responding to crises on their campuses. The scenarios include a variety of crises that occur on college campuses. The authors were asked to provide a personal reflection on the crisis and describe how it affected the campus, the staff, the students and their families, and the responders.

The authors freely share personal feelings and doubts about what was done and what else could have been done. They also share their passion for helping students and their families during these times. They demonstrate the concept of "sinning bravely," when a humane response is needed without concern for the institution's image or potential lawsuits.

We hope readers will appreciate the difficult and gut-wrenching decisions made by crisis responders and student affairs administrators in times of crisis. The size and location of an institution, the institutional culture, and its leadership greatly affect the response to crisis. In the scenarios that follow, the responses may differ, but the concern for affected students and their families is a constant.

Students Killed in Van Accident

Edward G. Whipple

By early spring 2002, I thought I had experienced enough student tragedy. During the first eight years of my tenure, beginning in 1994, we had developed a crisis intervention program, and in one three-year period, we had experienced 23 student deaths, including a murder, auto accidents, suicides, and natural deaths. Staff had become quite adept at working with students, families, and university faculty and staff in responding to tragic situations. I thought I had seen it all, but in March 2002, six Bowling Green State University undergraduates were killed in an accident on Interstate 75 in northern Kentucky. The young women were on their way back to Ohio after spending spring break in Florida. Five were suitemates in one of the university residence halls; the sixth also lived in the hall. The police report indicated that they were driving through a severe rainstorm when their van went into a skid and crossed the median into the path of an oncoming semitruck. All six were killed instantly.

Because the women were carrying university identification, the Kentucky State Highway Patrol quickly notified the university police. Our police contacted the associate dean of students, who coordinates our crisis plan.

I will never forget that phone call at 4:00 a.m., the last Saturday of spring break. As I picked up the phone, I knew something was wrong, but I did not think it was related to the university, because we were still on break. The associate dean said, "We've lost six students." My first questions were, "Who were the students? What happened? When? Where? Have the families been notified?" I felt increasingly sicker, and my thoughts vacillated between "what a horrendous waste" and "my God, their families."

I had no idea who might be on the campus, but it turned out that all the members of the crisis team were in town. Even the residence hall director had returned the day before to catch up on some work while it was still quiet. Before the crisis team meeting, I called the provost and the president, both of whom were out of town. They were shocked at the news and said they would return to campus as soon as possible.

The dean of students convened the meeting that early, very dreary Saturday morning. This group included the director of residence life, the director of the counseling center, the university police chief, the associate vice president for student affairs, the director of student health, and one of the vice provosts for academic affairs. In addition, the university attorney and director of marketing and communications were included on the team. One of the great things about working at my institution is that staff members have strong relationships with each other. In dealing with this terrible situation, we were aided by our history of working with each other on many other kinds of issues. Also, most of us had strong personal ties outside work, so we knew each others' personalities and how to work together during tense times. For example, the university attorney had a wonderful understanding of students, parents, and relationships. She was a key person in helping us discuss how to navigate through all the personal, legal, and public relations issues related to this accident. Our associate vice president for marketing and communications, the university's senior spokesperson, was a mother of three children, the oldest a university student. She was instrumental in helping us craft informative yet sensitive messages to the campus community and the media.

At the initial meeting, the crisis team focused on several major issues. These included positive identification of the students, family support, student support, and media control. At least one potentially terrible mistake was averted. One of the women who had been killed had the exact same name as another resident in the hall. It took some time, but calls among the state police, university police, and residence life resolved the confusion.

The team agreed that it was crucial for the university to contact the families. As a vice president, I have had to make my share of tough phone calls to parents, but I dreaded these. The associate vice president for student affairs—always a voice of reason in a crisis—said that he wanted to call the families on behalf of the university, and I was happy to let him do it. In retrospect, I was somewhat angry with myself for not making the calls myself, as I realized that this was not about my feelings but about the families and their feelings. In a similar situation (which I hope never occurs), I will make those calls.

We then focused our attention on how to deal with the residence hall students on their return the next day. The director of residence life and the director of the counseling center developed a plan that included a standard message regarding the accident. We called resident advisors to alert them about the accident and ask them to return to campus as soon as possible. When they did return, many were in shock. These students had been extremely popular in the hall and, as sophomores, were involved in many organizations on campus, including various clubs, sororities, and music ensembles. One student death hits hard; six are unimaginable. The crisis team planned and coordinated support services for students who knew the victims (and even for those who didn't), including counseling and contact with campus ministries.

Many students heard about the deaths on Sunday morning, as the news was on all local and regional television stations and in the newspapers. When they returned to the residence hall that day, they found it surrounded by television cameras, trucks with satellite dishes, and reporters trying to interview students. The university public relations staff did an excellent job of trying to handle the media, but I was angry that the students were being subjected to this. And as the media coverage became more intense, even students who did not know the women became distraught.

Following the young women's funeral services, which were all held the week after the accident, the residence hall council suggested a campuswide memorial service. I thought it was an excellent idea, as it would provide some closure for the community. The students planned the service, with advising support from the director of residence life and the dean of students. I hosted a dinner for the families before the service. What I thought would be a small group turned out to be more than 100 family members of the six women. It was an extremely moving time with the families. The president greeted each family and spoke with them privately before dinner. The service was held in the basketball arena, which was filled nearly to capacity on a snowy night. For me, the sight of six huge photographs on the stage—of these vibrant, beautiful young women—was almost too much. Between performances by several university choirs and family members speaking, it was an emotional event. I was amazed at how appreciative the families were to have the university honor their daughters. Many tears and embraces were shared after the service. The media were out in full force, but we did not allow them to televise or tape any part of the service.

A year later, the residence hall students dedicated a beautiful garden outside the hall to honor the women. Our development staff had worked with the students to raise the money, and facilities staff donated their time to help create the garden. Family members were invited to campus for the dedication, and I again hosted a meal. While it was not nearly as emotional and sad as the dinner the year before, there were a fair amount of tears. But I felt that the tears were more in celebration of the time these women had with us and how they had touched so many lives. Also, I felt that they were tears of thanks for a university community that showed its caring and support for its members.

I am not sure that the institution has totally recovered from this tragedy. We are a tight-knit community, with a large residential population. People know and care about each other. Several weeks after the memorial service, we made a thorough evaluation of our crisis plan and discussed our response to the tragedy; this was a major first step in recovery. Ongoing communication with each member of the crisis team over the next several months helped to address feelings. Checking in with each other, grieving together, and participating in structured debriefing opportunities for all involved were important. Finally, I am fortunate to work with an excellent counseling staff that provides wonderful outreach to students in the residence halls and fraternities and sororities. After the tragedy, they increased their programming efforts the rest of that semester, in addition to revamping their training for the many full-time staff and graduate students who work in living units.

As a vice president, I learned more than ever that I need to support my staff in crisis situations and let them work on doing what they know best how to do. In reflecting on my role, I simply tried to ensure that our management systems were in place, people were communicating, and decisions were being made quickly. My goal was to act on requests and remove institutional barriers for the people who were working closely with the families and students. The terrible tragedy reinforced my belief in trusting my own instincts to make decisions about when and how to respond in a tense situation. I also realized that I needed to trust the established processes and practices the university had in place for dealing with crises. Over time, and through constant evaluation, we had developed an effective system that could respond to different kinds of crises.

It was important for me to take care of the staff involved in the response. I had an obligation to tell responders who might be questioning their own ways of doing things, "Go ahead and trust your feelings and instincts." Also, I had to help them understand that they needed rest and it was okay to step back from the situation to pay attention to their own needs. Finally, this tragedy has reinforced my belief in the power and worth of common sense—no amount of process and protocol will take its place.

The Gainesville Murders

Arthur Sandeen

In more than three decades as a student affairs administrator, I responded to many crises. I worked at very large residential universities with socially active and academically competitive students. The campus environment was friendly but intense, and the drive to succeed among the students led to considerable stress. In hiring professional staff members over many years, I sought people who understood this volatile campus environment and had demonstrated an ability to respond effectively to crises. Being a senior student affairs administrator is a wonderful opportunity to serve, but it is not a position for people who want to avoid pressure, public criticism, long hours, or difficult decisions.

After having served as dean of students for six years and vice president for student affairs for 17 years, I thought I had experienced every difficult kind of crisis one could face in higher education. But in late August 1990, only a day before fall semester classes began at the University of Florida, a recently released convict from a Louisiana prison took the Gainesville exit off Interstate 75 and came to our campus. In the next three days, he brutally murdered four female students and one male student, all of whom lived in private apartments only a mile from the campus. These terrible murders immediately became national news, and we faced the worst crisis in the history of the institution. Parents, legislators, and others suggested that the university close for the semester and send the students home. The situation was made all the more difficult as the murderer was still at large; in fact, he was not captured until almost seven months later.

There was no precedent for this situation and no boilerplate response plan to address such a crisis. When the bodies of two female students were discovered in an off-campus apartment, I was the first campus official called by the police at 6:30 p.m. on Sunday. I immediately called the dean of students, and we went to the apartment complex. We remained there until well after midnight, having summoned about 15 other student affairs staff to the site to counsel students who lived in the large complex. We agreed to convene a group of about 20 campus and community leaders at 7:00 a.m. on Monday. Throughout the evening, I was in frequent contact with our president, provost, and other vice presidents. The group that met on Monday morning became the official coordinating team for this crisis, which only became worse as another female student was found dead in the same complex that day. On Wednesday, two more students were found murdered.

Our coordinating group was inclusive, with student leaders, faculty, student affairs staff, clergy, academic administrators, police, attorneys, counselors, campus and city police, elected officials, and public relations officers. All our sessions were open, and members of the press often were present. We had the complete support of the president, and when financial resources were needed, the university, its foundation, and the community provided them. Our group met frequently, and all actions, responses, and policies were the result of our discussions. The coordinating group continued to meet for the next eight months.

Because I was the senior student affairs officer at the institution, it never occurred to me that I should not be the one to convene such a group and serve as its chair. I had handled many other campus crises during my career, and I assumed that I was expected to take this leadership role.

Probably because I had been very aggressive in handling difficult student crises for the institution in the past, others seemed to accept my actions in this crisis. It is not up to me to say whether what we did in this situation was right, or humane, or in the best interests of the victims' families or of the institution. My purpose here is not to debate the quality of the response we made but to describe the balancing of responsibilities and feelings in such a situation.

I now have the perspective of 15 years since these terrible murders took place, but the feelings are still with me. This experience, by far the most difficult of my life, left a permanent scar on my heart. It will be part of my consciousness forever, as it will be for the thousands of University of Florida students, faculty, alumni, and community members who were here during that difficult time.

I suspect that, for some of us, assuming a major leadership responsibility in a crisis is in itself a means of coping. For better or worse, I have always responded to problems with action. I had no doubt what my responsibility was in this situation, and I knew that I would have to call on every skill and bit of energy I had to do my job. Like everyone else, I was aghast at the details of the murders and the loss of five young and promising students, and I had to work hard to maintain my composure and suppress my emotions. And, like other professional staff involved in this situation, I was not able to mask my feelings at all times. The emotional overload we experienced caused some staff members to back away from the crisis, for a few hours or a few days. Luckily, there was enough support among our staff that private bursts of anger, fear, frustration, and tears were understood and tolerated.

I had the dubious advantage of having responded to many student deaths over the years, so I knew what I had to do to maintain some kind of balance between my responsibilities and my feelings. Despite the pressure and the time demands, I continued to eat well, sleep at least seven hours a night, and get some physical exercise each day. Being the senior student affairs officer at a large institution can be very draining physically and emotionally; for many years, my major way of coping was through regular, vigorous exercise (playing squash), healthy eating, and sufficient rest. This case placed demands on me that were unceasing in terms of time, public exposure, criticism, and pressure. I knew that if I were going to be able to provide leadership during the long crisis, I had to maintain my own physical and mental health.

It is also necessary for the senior student affairs officer to pay close attention to the student affairs staff during such a crisis. Just because these people are trained professionals does not mean that they are immune to the emotional problems others experience. Indeed, one of the mistakes we made during these many weeks was to focus our efforts almost exclusively on students. We should have paid more attention to the feelings and mental health of our own staff, and other faculty and staff in the institution. One of the reactions people had to these serial murders was denial—the events were so traumatic that some people tried to dismiss them from their minds and not deal with their feelings. After a few weeks, however, the feelings of fear, anger, and sorrow emerged, and the demands on our helping services on campus became almost overwhelming.

The community was desperate for some closure on these horrible crimes but was constantly reminded in the press and on television that the murderer was still at large. Thus, we had to maintain a balance between our responsibilities and our feelings for several months. The coordinating committee expanded, and we found that by sharing observations and feelings within that group, we were able to focus on newly identified needs and cope with our own feelings.

A person who is not affected by a tragedy such as this would not be human. Some student affairs staff will not be able to cope effectively with such crises, and they should be assured that this is acceptable. Not everyone is equal to the task. But the senior student affairs officer is clearly expected to assume a leadership role and to ensure that the institution's response is timely, humane, and sensitive. The best way to do this is to deal openly with one's own feelings, share them with others, pay careful attention to the needs of professional staff, and take care of one's own physical and mental health during the crisis.

A 57-Foot Wall of Water, 20 Miles Offshore

James E. Martin

As we huddled in the dark around the emergency broadcast radio, we heard the chilling news that a 57-foot wall of water was racing toward our community of Pensacola, Florida. It was September 16, 2004, and Pensacola Junior College was abandoned except for the evacuees who had sought safety in its block-reinforced buildings. Hurricane Ivan was a monster in the Gulf of Mexico, heading toward landfall in Florida or Alabama. My family and I, and our dog, had left our home in Gulf Breeze, Florida, 12 hours earlier. We lived on a barrier island and had been told to evacuate or provide police officials with the names of our next of kin. My wife and I, along with our 13-year-old daughter and 11- and 8-year-old sons, decided to "ride out the storm" in my office on the Pensacola campus. Equipped with sleeping bags, air mattresses, rations, flashlights, and an emergency radio, we awaited the unknown.

For over a week, forecasters had tracked the progress of Hurricane Ivan as it traversed the Atlantic Ocean and the Caribbean Sea, then moved into the Gulf of Mexico. The Pensacola area had not experienced a major hurricane or tropical storm for 10 years, and our community hoped against hope that the storm would veer off in another direction. However, as the hurricane track became more defined, it was obvious that Pensacola was going to be directly hit or at least severely impacted by a Category 4 or 5 hurricane.

Pensacola Junior College, a public community college in the Florida Community College System, had begun implementing its preparedness procedures two days before the hurricane struck. Employees were told to move any electrical equipment away from windows, cover all computers and other sensitive equipment with black garbage bags, close all blinds, and go home to take care of their families. Classes were dismissed one day before the hurricane was to arrive. The president and two vice presidents moved into their offices on campus, partially to seek shelter but also so they would be there to oversee recovery efforts when the hurricane had passed. The school gym had been designated as a "special needs shelter" for Escambia County, Florida. (A special needs shelter is an evacuation site for people who have special medical or personal needs.) By the time Hurricane Ivan made landfall, Pensacola Junior College was home to nearly 300 evacuees who needed special medical treatment.

My family and I had never been required to evacuate. Our home is located in an area about one-quarter mile from Escambia Bay and 1.5 miles from Santa Rosa Sound. As we packed precious belongings such as photo albums, videotapes of the children in the earlier years, family heirlooms, and those special teddy bears and "irreplaceable toys" in the cars, my wife and I did not know what we would find when we returned. We had boarded up all the windows and doors with reinforced plywood. We placed as much furniture on beds as possible, in the event that a storm surge from the bay or the sound flooded the house. As we left, my wife and I had an uncertain feeling about the future of our home. It was very quiet in the two cars as we drove away.

Law enforcement officers lined the highway from our community to Pensacola. The two bridges leading from our barrier island would soon be closed. Some people had elected to stay on the island to ride out the storm, a decision that proved fatal for some of them.

During the daylight hours of September 16, my children played hide-and-seek in the large administrative building. They took turns taking Mandy, our West Highland terrier, for walks around campus. Storm clouds, rain, and squally winds increased as the day progressed. My wife and I reassured the children that they were safe and we would soon be returning to our home. I ventured to another administrative building to talk with the president and another vice president. We made plans to meet at daylight the next morning. As darkness fell on campus, the winds and rain began to increase. Air flights into and out of Pensacola ceased around 6:00 p.m., and the highways were finally cleared of the trail of evacuees heading out of town to avoid the approaching storm.

We inflated our air mattresses and opened our sleeping bags. Shortly after darkness fell, we lost power. We broke out flashlights and the emergency broadcast radio. Local radio stations in Florida and Alabama continued to report the latest hurricane coordinates. Initially, the storm appeared to be heading toward the Mobile Bay (Alabama) area, which would mean somewhat of a reprieve for Pensacola. With the children playing flashlight tag, my wife and I huddled next to the radio, listening for the latest details on the projected track of the massive storm. Winds were now sustained at 135 mph, and a storm surge of 15 feet was predicted. As the winds increased and the rain began pounding against the windows of my second-floor office, we decided to move our "campsite" to the first floor. I began to fear that the roof would fly off, and I wanted my family as low in the building as possible.

One by one, the local radio stations were knocked off the air by the high winds. Our emergency radio was now receiving reports only from the Mobile emergency broadcast system. At about 9:30 p.m., the National Weather Service reported that the hurricane had taken a jog to the east, meaning that Pensacola was going to receive a direct hit from this massive storm. For the first time, my wife and I feared for the safety of our family. I knew that my campus building was sturdy, but could it withstand sustained 135 mph winds and the expected tornados? The building had four first-floor entrances—we set up our campsite in the corridor in the center of the building, away from all glass doors. We looked for interior rooms that could possibly survive damage to the structure. Campus police came in long enough to get the names of those staying in the building and the names of our next of kin. Only my wife and I recognized the gravity of their questions. The children, fairly oblivious to the approaching danger, were beginning to settle down for a "campout in Daddy's building." The two older children bedded down about 20 feet from us; the youngest wanted to be "next to Mom and Dad." Amazingly, they all fell asleep; my wife and I continued to listen to the lone emergency broadcast station. At about midnight, the station reported that a buoy 20 miles offshore in the Gulf of Mexico had recorded a 57-foot wave heading toward Pensacola. We looked at each other, knowing that we were safe from the approaching storm surge but that our home was in peril.

People who experience hurricanes and tornados usually describe the winds as sounding "like a freight train." The howl of the wind outside my office building didn't sound like a freight train to me; it sounded more like a jet engine racing down a runway for takeoff. My wife and I lay in our sleeping bags, but neither of us slept. Suddenly, all the glass doors began to vibrate and rattle, as if someone were pulling on them from the outside. The noise awakened the children. We told them that they were safe, that it was only the wind. Occasionally, we would venture toward one of the doors and peer outside into the darkness, trying to see what was going on. The wind-driven rain prevented us from seeing the destruction that was occurring on campus. Suddenly, there was a loud crash as a large object struck the side of the building. Not until daylight did we know that one of the 400-pound air-conditioner chillers had been blown off the roof of the building next door. Throughout the night, we listened to the deafening sounds of howling wind and rain. Daylight presented a surreal picture of the campus. We cautiously ventured out of the building and saw classrooms with roofs torn off, brick walls blown down, shattered windows, and more than 200 trees toppled or snapped in half. One could easily track the path of a tornado by the damage it had inflicted. The scent of fresh pine filled the air. As we walked around, we saw large commercial signs blown onto the campus from adjacent malls and shopping centers. Cars floated in parking lots. This devastated campus would be our home for two more days.

While we were there, a student appeared in the midst of the destruction and rubble. He wanted to know when classes would resume. It was obvious that the college would not reopen for quite awhile, but he wanted to resume his classes. Another student confronted me, wanting to know when his student financial aid check would be available. His family was hungry and he needed money.

There was no access to our community: Bridges leading to our home were severely damaged, and the governor's office had ordered inspections and repairs. Raw sewage had been swept into the city of Pensacola over an area of nearly eight blocks, and the smell was overpowering. The campus was still without power or water.

Three hundred Florida National Guardsmen were camped out on the campus. Their presence was reassuring, since there were reports of some looting in the area. The guardsmen were polite and sensitive guests on our campus, and they brought fresh water.

Finally, after two days, we were told that we could return to Gulf Breeze. However, the bridges were still deemed to be unsafe, so we had to drive an extra 55 miles to get home. Home. What would we find? During the trip, we saw incredible destruction of property. The storm surge had washed houses and people out to sea. My children were uncharacteristically silent as we drove through the neighborhoods of newly homeless people. As we neared our home, we grew more apprehensive. We turned the corner and saw our house, still standing but with obvious roof and screen enclosure damage. Our neighborhood, like Pensacola Junior College, was without power. We had ordered a gas-powered generator before the hurricane, but it did not arrive in time for the power outages. Neighbors with generators provided light and temporary air-conditioning for our family. We bathed in our swimming pool.

At the college, the administrative team began to assemble. I was told to report back to campus at 8:00 the next morning to begin assessing damage and checking on the status of our staff members. Leaving my family behind, I drove to the bridge that connects Gulf Breeze to Pensacola. The National Guardsman directing traffic away from the bridge reluctantly permitted me to traverse the three-mile-long bridge with the following disclaimer: "I won't be responsible for your safety while you're on the bridge." A Gulf Breeze City Police car, with blue lights flashing, cautiously led me across. Instinctively, I rolled all the windows down, in case a section of the bridge collapsed under the weight of my car. I could see the blue flashing lights of police cars on the other side. I had this same escort across the bridge for the next three days.

As the administrative team gathered, it was apparent that the storm had taken an emotional and physical toll on the PJC staff. The homes of 31 PJC staff members were either totally destroyed or uninhabitable. Many of those staff members were sitting around the table with me as we talked about reopening the college. Many were wearing the only clothes they were able to salvage from their destroyed homes. Unselfishly, they were on campus to help with the restoration of the college, temporarily delaying the process of finding homes for their own families. There were tales of bravery and frustration, expressions of anger and disbelief, and tears and laughter. The meeting was an emotional event for our administrative team. However, none of us was prepared to hear that we had lost a member of the PJC community. A recently retired librarian died when the surging waters trapped her in her home. Her body was found in her front yard by law enforcement officials. We were all deeply saddened that one of our colleagues had lost her life in the hurricane. Ultimately, she would be one of 21 storm-related deaths in our community.

The administrative team met every day at 8:00 a.m. to discuss the progress of rebuilding our physical plant and ensuring that the PJC human community was intact. After three weeks, Pensacola Junior College reopened for classes; however, approximately 800 students withdrew for hurricane-related reasons. Many had lost their homes; some had lost their jobs; others had lost their means of transportation. In nearly all instances, the college refunded tuition and fees.

Hurricane Ivan was a devastating event in the life of Pensacola Junior College and the lives of members of the PJC community. However, the hurricane provided the community with a sense of cohesiveness and perseverance.

Managing Communicable Diseases

Lora L. Jasman and Larry D. Roper

Context of the Incident

A student who was infected with measles joined 14 companions to travel from their home country in Asia to attend an English Language Institute (ELI) summer program at Oregon State University (OSU) in August 2003. The student became ill with a fever before leaving the country and was seen by a physician at the departure airport. The physician failed to diagnose measles and approved the student for travel. The student became increasingly ill during the flight and was attended by a physician on board, who suspected measles. When the plane landed in San Francisco, the student was transported by ambulance to a hospital. The emergency room physician did not think the condition was measles and released the student, who immediately boarded a flight to Portland, Oregon. (ELI is housed at Oregon State University. ELI students are not officially considered OSU students; however, they are eligible to live in OSU residence halls and participate in campus activities. In our work and problem-solving with community health agencies, we make no distinction between OSU and ELI.)

In Portland, the student and his 14 traveling companions were met by OSU program staff, who noted that he was ill and had "spots on his hands." They were reassured when they learned that he had been evaluated by three physicians. The group was transported to Corvallis on a chartered bus. The next morning, program staff received a phone call from a physician in San Francisco, where the student had been seen in the emergency department, following up on the condition of the student and recommending that he be reevaluated.

The student had come for a one-month language program and had not paid the fees required for access to OSU Student Health Services (SHS), so the staff members called the health center for advice. Because of limited summer staffing and the possible need for isolation procedures, the health center physician worked with the local county health department communicable disease nurse to arrange for medical evaluation in an isolation room at the local hospital, where an infectious disease specialist gave a likely diagnosis of measles and ordered blood tests for confirmation.

The next day, the student was released from the hospital. Because of the time that had elapsed since he first became ill, he was no longer considered contagious; however, the exposure of others to the infected student posed public health concerns.

Since most of the 14 student companions who were contacts to the patient spoke limited English, health department personnel used a commercial telephone translation line to interview all the patient's contacts to determine their measles history and vaccination status. A total of 18 contacts (14 Asian companions and four program staff members) were identified, located, and interviewed. Many of them did not know their medical history and immunization status, so health department personnel made arrangements for international telephone calls to elicit this information from parents. It was determined that 16 of the 18 contacts should receive a measles vaccine because they were lacking a history of full immunity (having neither a history of prior disease nor documentation of *two* prior measles vaccines—although most gave a history of one prior vaccine.) The contacts were within a 72-hour window of exposure, so health department personnel obtained consent and administered the MMR (measles, mumps, and rubella) vaccine to these individuals. Of greatest concern was one student who was thought to be completely unprotected. Select members of the SARS (severe acute respiratory syndrome) task force that had been convening for about a year, together with ELI and housing services staff, met to discuss the situation, develop a communication plan, and consult with the Oregon Department of Human Services (DHS) and the Centers for Disease Control and Prevention (CDC). Housing and food services personnel were asked to make arrangements for a possible quarantine.

OSU housing personnel made the decision to move the entire traveling group from a residence hall to a much smaller cooperative residence facility (40-person house) that was vacant for the summer. The facility was cleaned and arrangements were made for meal service. Everyone outside the original travel group who would enter the building was required to have immunity against measles. Health officials from the local health department and OSU prepared a news release and media talking points; the director of the student health center would be the media contact.

Once the lab had confirmed the initial case of measles, the county health department, OSU, and DHS implemented the quarantine plan for the student who had no history of immunity. The agencies stayed in contact throughout the weekend to deal with increasing media interest.

Medical textbooks indicate that the incubation period for measles (the time between exposure and onset of disease) averages about 10 days but can range from 7 to 18 days. An incubation period as short as 7 days is rare. The DHS and CDC experts said they felt "very comfortable" beginning the quarantine on day 8 so that it would not disrupt the student's weekend with her host family. We questioned the wisdom of this decision because of the possibility of a shorter incubation period, but ultimately it seemed like a reasonable compromise that would both protect the public and allow as much freedom as possible for the student.

On Monday, while under conditions of quarantine, the student without known immunity developed a headache and fever; we watched her closely for symptoms of measles. Over the next two days, typical measles spots began to develop; unfortunately, this student (Case 2) fell into the rare category of developing measles after a very short incubation period (7 days). We then had to trace all the contacts she had potentially exposed when she attended a religious service and a potluck over the weekend with her host family.

Unlike the first student (Case 1), who tolerated measles fairly well, the second student became quite ill. To maintain isolation, ELI program assistants cared for her in rotating shifts in her room at the cooperative residence. After several days, she continued to have a high fever and began to have difficulty maintaining hydration, so we made arrangements to take her to the student health center on a Saturday, when the center was otherwise closed for intravenous hydration. Her condition persisted and she eventually required several days of hospitalization.

Fortunately, there were no more cases. In the end, the county health department identified a total of 155 contacts and had been able to reach more than 90 percent of them. The personnel costs to the county and university for managing the incident were significant, although actual costs were not calculated.

Response and Lessons Learned

: Create a permanent response team.

We learned that a key component in an effective communicable disease response is the development of a permanent team. Core members on our team, which we now call the Infectious Diseases Response Team (IDRT), included representatives from student health services, university environmental health department, news and communications, housing and dining services, residence life, Greek life, summer session (which offers short-term summer courses), international education, ELI, registrar's office, and public safety, as well as communicable disease personnel from the local health department.

We were thankful that many members of the team already had good working relationships through their previous work on the SARS task force. Mutual trust and camaraderie are particularly helpful in making decisions for a communicable disease response. We had prepared for a possible SARS outbreak, and many of the decision-making principles were similar. This allowed us to respond quickly to this incident and brought home the importance of having a team that meets regularly, has established relationships, and plans in advance. Members of the IDRT are comfortable knowing that if they are faced with a similar incident, they will have the tools to make informed decisions and will not feel alone.

Lesson #2: Agree in advance on how decisions will be made.

We learned the hard way that a team is not effective unless basic agreements are in place about how decisions will be made. Unfortunately, at the time of the measles outbreak on our campus, we had not developed these agreements.

Each member of the team came with a unique perspective, which was both beneficial and a potential source of conflict. Members from international education and ELI were concerned about treating the international students well and minimizing the stigma they would feel. They made passionate appeals such as, "These students have paid a lot of money to come to the United States to get a great international experience. We can't lock them up in a poorly cleaned housing unit and tell them they can't go anywhere!" Representatives from housing and dining facilities wished to quarantine the group immediately—their concern was for the safety of other people in the residence halls who might be exposed. Health care practitioners were most concerned about treating the infected student and limiting the spread of infection. These conflicting agendas made it difficult to agree on when and for how long our unimmunized student should be quarantined.

To help us resolve the issue, we sought the advice of outside health care experts at the CDC and the Oregon DHS. These experts were comfortable with a plan that would allow the at-risk student to spend a weekend with her host family before she was quarantined on day 8. Several of the health care workers on our team questioned the wisdom of this plan, recommending instead that we start the quarantine on day 7. But instead of following our instincts, we agreed to the compromise. In retrospect, we paid a high price, as our student (Case 2) was one of the rare patients who had a shorter incubation period. Several of us regretted that we hadn't been more forceful about starting the quarantine earlier.

As a result of this experience, we developed the following key decision-making principles to enable us to do better in future incidents:

1. It is the local health department, health care providers, and university officials who must deal with any communicable disease outbreak and who must accept the ramifications of their work. Decisions involving limitations on freedom of movement and freedom of choice are sure to be contentious, even among professionals. Our highest priority is to safeguard public health.

2. In all future work, we will use the most conservative authoritative medical and epidemiological evidence when faced with a range of possible actions. The lack of scientific certainty or consensus must not be used to postpone preventive action in the face of a threat to public safety.

3. Consultation with state or national experts is recommended and can be extremely useful. However, we have decided to make final decisions locally. (If we had quarantined the second student earlier, we could have eliminated virtually all exposures to her.)

4. We are committed to protecting the right of confidentiality for the involved students despite pressure to give out information.

Lesson #3: Use sound medical information to determine the limits of exposure.

Some members of our team were confused about who needed to be quarantined and which contacts were vulnerable. When the visiting students first arrived at OSU, they were scheduled to stay in a residence hall that was also hosting a large group of older people attending an educational program. Residence hall personnel who learned of the situation initially assumed that these healthy older people were highly vulnerable because of their age; on the contrary, they were actually at low risk because most of them had probably had measles as children. The lack of clarity about contagion created significant anxiety for residence hall personnel, who were frightened not only for the residents but also for themselves and their families.

It ultimately worked well for us to assume that healthy persons who had been in contact with the students who had measles were adequately protected if they had received two measles vaccines (even if the second was within 72 hours of exposure) or had been born before 1957 (the immunization standard for all OSU students). This decision, based on sound medical information, allowed us to more easily determine who could safely travel about and who needed to be restricted. It was very reassuring to staff when we were able to definitively say they were not at risk.

However, we had some difficulty determining immunity status for all the contacts. For example, some of the student employees who were asked to clean the quarantine facility were new students, and their immunization data were not yet easily retrievable. Some of the closest contacts were anxious because they weren't absolutely certain of their immunity status—we were surprised at the number of health care workers who were unsure of their measles immunity status. One health care worker who had been in close contact with one of the ill students was born before 1957 but was concerned because she hadn't been immunized against measles and had never had the disease. To reassure her, we tested her and confirmed that she did have immunity, but that decision was made after she had already spent considerable time with the ill student.

At one point, we contacted a home health nursing agency to see if it could assist with the ill student, but the agency declined to help because its employees were all born after 1957 and the agency had no documented measles immunization history for them. It was disconcerting to us that an agency that seemed most appropriate to help in this medical situation was unwilling. Even hospital staff were initially a bit reluctant to provide assistance, given the exposure ramifications. We identified and documented these problems so we could address them at a later date.

Lesson #4: Expect discomfort in information dissemination and control.

It is unlikely that any leader in an infectious disease crisis situation will feel completely comfortable with information control and dissemination. In our situation, dozens of people had access to at least some of the information, and the involved students were free to share information with anyone they chose. We were greatly concerned about the accuracy of information being released to the news media. In fact, someone sent an anonymous e-mail to the local media suggesting the possibility that we had SARS on our campus, because the infected students were from an Asian country.

Dissemination of information was delayed within the university itself. The incident occurred in the summer, when staffing was low, so only a few people were notified early on. The director of the health center had been on vacation and didn't learn about it until the second day. It took some time to determine the full extent of the problem and to interview close contacts of Case 1 to determine whether they had been immunized. Obtaining contact information was especially difficult because the students didn't speak English well.

We found that there is a common desire to want more complete information before triggering an infectious diseases crisis response; that is, convening a communicable disease response team to discuss management and communication plans for an incident. In the case of infectious disease, getting more complete medical information can take days—even weeks—while TV and newspaper reporters are on the line within hours! Some of us wished we could hide until we had more clarity about how to manage the situation; ironically, we discovered that clarity came only as we convened and openly talked about the areas where it was lacking. The director of the health center felt somewhat unprepared to provide answers to specific questions and embarrassed about her lack of firsthand knowledge about measles, as she had never treated a case. (In fact, most physicians in the United States have never seen a patient with measles, as only about 100 cases are reported annually.) The director openly admitted her lack of knowledge and sought information from reference resources and discussions with experienced colleagues.

We felt significant pressure not to "embarrass the institution" by managing the situation poorly or providing damaging information to the media. Most top administrators wanted to be informed but not involved. We were committed to doing our job well so they did not have to be involved, but we definitely experienced anxiety about the responsibility.

Lesson #5: Promote leadership in all parts of the organization.

It is not always obvious who should make the decision to trigger a communicable disease crisis response, or when. Medical practitioners, who are trained to diagnose and treat patients, aren't always trained to think about the broader picture, including communication of risk to the public through the media. People who are closely connected to the situation may underestimate the impact of information they provide to the university or the larger community.

We have found that it is important to create a communication system in which people at multiple levels are responsible for thinking about the big picture. Relying on a single person, such as the director or medical director of the student health service, to trigger a communicable disease crisis response could be problematic. Depending on the nature of the situation, some people are more likely than others to even pose the question, "Should we prepare for a greater impact on the community?" We have decided that the recommendation to convene the response team to discuss a potential infectious disease crisis may come from any member of our response team or from outside the team.

This approach requires a certain amount of humility, especially among medical leaders. Medical personnel are most likely to be expected, by themselves and others, to decide when to convene a team for an infectious disease crisis response. But, for the reasons listed above, they aren't always the first to recognize the need. This is where members of a team can work together to ensure that gaps are covered and action is taken that is in the best interest of the persons at risk, the university, and the surrounding community.

Lesson #6: Develop methods for timely and ongoing communication.
Maintaining communication among members of the team and others affected by the situation was critical to our infectious disease response. E-mail and conference calls were useful for ensuring adequate patient care, clear communication, coordinated planning, and consistent public information release. E-mail was used for routine information, but for strategizing and decision making, we found conference calls to be the most useful and practical method. With only an hour's notice, we could convene at least four or five members of the team for a 30-minute conference call. We used conference calls to clarify issues, maintain an equal understanding of the information at hand, identify a spokesperson, develop talking points for dealing with media inquiries, and determine a course of action.

Throughout the early days of the crisis, it was necessary to physically convene available members at least once a day and sometimes twice. These meetings promoted teamwork and a sense of trust and support within the team. As much as possible, university team members tried to meet at a single location and conference others in through a speakerphone.

One problem was a lack of knowledgeable backup personnel. The incident occurred during the summer, when many staff members had scheduled vacations or days off, and the surveillance required for possible new cases was more than six weeks. Sometimes days or even weeks went by with no need for the team members to communicate, giving a false impression that the crisis was over. But then, suddenly, another issue would surface. For example, three weeks after the beginning of the quarantine period, a third student became ill, and we were concerned that he might be developing measles. At this point, several members of the team were on vacation, and their backups had either not been identified to the rest of the team or had not been adequately briefed. We were relieved when this student did not develop measles, but we were disturbed at our complacency in not adequately designating and briefing backups. We had discussed the subject early on in the incident but had not followed up. Continued vigilance during the lengthy infectious disease incident was fatiguing, and in a time of relative calm it was all too easy to let some of the details slide.

Another problem we encountered was the unanticipated need to communicate with members of the team after hours and on weekends. Although we had exchanged business numbers, we didn't have at our fingertips the home and cell phone numbers of all members of the team, or some of us had the information at work but then needed it at home. Part of the reason for this lack of planning was that we made some assumptions about how the situation would evolve, and we had not yet learned to expect the unexpected. For example, we expected to be contacted by the media only at work, but sometimes we were contacted at home. We expected medical results to be available on a certain weekday, but they came through on the weekend. And the students sometimes became ill, or more ill, in the evening hours. Occasionally, we became frustrated about our lack of planning, but in retrospect we realized that our mistakes showed us the holes in our response plan, so we could do a better job in the future.

Several members of the Infectious Diseases Response Team who were most likely to respond to media questions had previously received some training in risk communication. There are well-researched and very practical ways to ease the outrage and concern of the public regarding communicable disease risk. We have used the work of Peter Sandman (www.psandman.com) to train our staff. Excellent information is also available from the U.S. Department of Health and Human Services at www.riskcommunication.samhsa.gov.

Lesson #7: Manage the emotional impact on the team and the community.
Dealing with disappointments, setbacks, and mistakes was far easier when the team was communicating regularly and collaborating in making decisions. The experience of working together to accomplish a common purpose led to camaraderie and support that kept the group pressing forward. Sharing frustrations, embarrassments, and mistakes relieved anxiety and often led to solutions. On one occasion, a member of our team was being interviewed by a newspaper reporter late in the evening. In trying to communicate that measles can be a very serious problem, she began by saying, "Many people might think, 'Measles? Whoop-de-do.'" She worried all night that this would actually be quoted in the newspaper. Sharing experiences and concerns within the group often led to learning for the entire group and sometimes provided some humor in the face of an otherwise serious and difficult situation.

Another challenge we faced was that the second student who developed measles became much sicker than we expected. She spoke little English, and we tried very hard to take care of her in the housing facility, where she would have familiar, friendly faces. Every day, our medical personnel checked on her and provided guidance to those caring for her. We expected to see improvement after the first few days, but she continued to have a fever and was unable to eat or drink. We made special arrangements to provide her with intravenous hydration at the health center, but she remained quite ill. We finally took her to the hospital. We wondered later if we had done the right thing in trying to keep her out of the hospital for so long. The continuous care took an emotional and physical toll on our volunteer caretakers. We found it helpful to debrief the incident afterward to encourage each other, thank the volunteers, and learn from the experience.

In a situation like this, emotions can run high in the greater university community. It can be challenging to find ways to address common concerns while also managing panic. We encouraged all team members to voice any concerns they had heard from students or employees in their areas. This was a good way to keep track of the general level of anxiety. We found that addressing every concern promptly with either information or suggested procedures made a huge difference.

Ongoing Work

As difficult as it is to deal with a communicable disease outbreak, the experience can motivate members of a university to prepare for the future. Ongoing planning has been critical for maintaining the IDRT relationships that are necessary to immediately respond to a crisis. We have encouraged the team to keep asking the question, "What if?" so we can identify weaknesses in our response plan. (For example, what if this situation had happened in the Greek system? What if the student lived off campus? What if it had happened during the academic term? What if more students had been affected? What if it had been SARS?) Through this line of questioning, we developed a "work in progress" response protocol, which is posted at: http://studenthealth.oregonstate.edu/topics/InfectiousDisease.php.

The team continues to strengthen its effort to ensure the healthy functioning of our community by:

- Supporting the growth and development of individuals on the team while promoting the health and well-being of the community as a whole.

- Managing the reciprocal relationship between the individual and the environment—attending to individual and public health concerns.

- Adopting sound policies and practices.

- Implementing comprehensive intervention strategies.

- Intervening in risky or threatening health situations.

- Building strong networks and partnerships to create and sustain healthy environments.

Recently, the team was effective in responding to legislation that proposed changes in immunization requirements. A bill in the Oregon legislature proposed that students attending universities on nonimmigrant visas be immunized against measles before attending classes rather than allowing the current one-term grace period. The IDRT was committed to thorough, respectful, and thoughtful analysis of the issues and was able to provide helpful language and guidance in the legislative process.

Since the measles incident, we have dealt with a pertussis (whooping cough) outbreak, a norovirus (Norwalk virus) outbreak, and a flu vaccine shortage, and have managed a situation in which a student had active tuberculosis. Each situation was different, and each has strengthened our commitment to promote community health through a caring, responsive, and respectful team partnership. Through our management of communicable disease incidents, we have become keenly aware that accepting our humanity, dealing with our emotional responses, and supporting each other are part of our collective responsibility.

Fatalities in a Residence Hall Fire

Dawn L. Williams

An intense fire occurred at approximately 4:30 a.m. this morning in a common area on the third floor of Boland Hall, on the campus of Seton Hall University. Boland Hall, which opened in 1952, is a residence hall for freshmen that houses approximately 600 students. The cause of the fire is under investigation by the Essex County Prosecutor's Office.

Three fatalities have been confirmed. Identification of the victims is pending. Fifty-four students, two South Orange firefighters and two South Orange police officers have been sent to area hospitals for injuries ranging from burns to smoke inhalation. Those hospitals include Saint Barnabas (Livingston), University Hospital (Newark), Newark Beth Israel (Newark), Orange Memorial (Orange), Overlook (Summit), Mountainside (Montclair), Saint Michael's (Newark), and East Orange General (East Orange) (Boland Hall Fire, 2000).

So reads the original announcement posted by the Seton Hall University media team regarding the fire on January 19, 2000. The announcement goes on to describe the state of the building's alarm system, including the dates of recent inspections. "The system was in proper working order and was used efficiently and effectively by firefighters" (Boland Hall Fire, 2000). The announcement includes an update on temporary housing for students who had been displaced by the fire and the hotline number for parents seeking information about their children.

This announcement is among the documents in a university Web site archive I examined in preparing to write this piece. These documents chronicle the facts as they unfolded in this tragedy, which changed the history of this Catholic university in South Orange, New Jersey. Reviewing these documents brought the experience vividly back to mind.

Much has changed. The university has installed/upgraded sprinkler systems in all residence halls, and most of the students who were freshman at the time of the fire have graduated. But every day we hear the chimes of the bells that were built in remembrance of the three students who died: Aaron Karol, Frank Caltibilota, and John Giunta. The university community holds a remembrance service each year on the anniversary of the fire. We hold a vigil around the remembrance stone that has been placed in the courtyard of Boland Hall. For many, there is no real knowledge of what occurred on this date. For some, there is a distant memory of the events that occurred immediately following the fire. The memory grows, and the emotions come rushing back. I am among this latter group. The experience changed me. I have moved on; but when I'm reminded of it, I feel the full impact all over again.

"On June 12, 2003, the Essex County Prosecutor's Office announced that the Grand Jury had issued indictments against several individuals for their alleged roles in the Boland Hall fire..." (Diamond, 2003). The trial of these persons continues as this book goes to press, and each time I read an update I am reminded of one of my most vivid emotions during the incident: anger. I recall the anger I felt for the lives that had been lost—those who died and those who started the fire. The lives of those who started the fire will be forever changed; they will live their entire lives with the consequences of their actions. We hope our students will never have to deal with fatal outcomes like these, but we know there will be those who will have to deal with such tragic consequences.

It is difficult to detach from the emotion of such an intense experience, but with time one is able to think about what one has learned. The experience brought together a community of people both within and outside the university to support those affected by the incident. Some people took on roles that were new to them; others continued their regular duties in a more visible way.

Creating a Community Space

As a private university, we were able to designate private spaces as well as areas that were public. Members of the press were escorted while they were on campus, with the understanding that some areas were off-limits to them. Some spaces and events were identified as private for the university community. The University Center was such a space. Students and others in the greater university community knew that this space was intended for "Seton Hall family only." It was a place where people could come for information, assistance, and relaxation. Later, students told us how much it meant to know that the University Center was one place they could go and not worry about the press following them to ask questions. It became a safe haven.

Because the University Center's main lounge was where students congregated for the first update, it was established as the location for regular updates. At the end of each update, the time of the next one was announced. These updates came to be known as "community gatherings"; they were led by King Mott, dean for freshman studies, and me. In the beginning, our purpose was to inform the university community of what we knew; but a secondary agenda came to be equally important: the coming together of the community for moral support.

We began the gathering with prayer and moved on to the facts as we knew them. We gave students instructions on next steps in terms of housing and let them know where they could pick up the clothing and toiletries they would need while they were out of the residence halls. We answered the questions we could and kept track of information we needed to get before the next update. We ended by announcing when the next gathering would be held. We closed in prayer.

The sessions could have been filled with expressions of anger over details that were not known. In fact, a few people started down that path, but it became clear that this was not the time for that. The questions could be answered later. This was a time for solace and community. As the days and weeks passed and many students temporarily moved to off-campus housing, the Internet became the primary source of information. I found that I missed the gatherings. There was a bond among us when we came together, an important bond that could not be duplicated through electronic communication.

Be Honest About What You Know

I learned that, as difficult as it is to say you have no additional information at this time, it is better to be honest than to create false hopes that are later shattered. Also, any inaccurate information you provide will jeopardize your overall credibility. What people need most in a crisis situation is to be able to trust what is being said.

Relying on the Kindness of Colleagues

Colleagues quickly began to come forward, in person and through e-mail and phone messages, to offer assistance. These were not colleagues whose job it was to respond to the incident but those who simply wanted to reach out and let us know that they understood what we were experiencing. The first person in my personal circle who came forth was a friend from the community who represented the local clergy association, offering assistance in finding homes in the community for students who had been displaced. By the end of the first day, we had members of the state psychological association helping with crisis counseling; psychologists from neighboring colleges assisting students; members of various residence life staffs making arrangements to relocate students; and a fellow dean of students helping to coordinate the collection of clothing donations. The actions of these volunteers confirmed the goodness of people and the support that existed in the surrounding community.

Personal Reactions

Everyone says this, and I will, too: As a responder, take time for yourself. Make certain that your family has a communication plan for the times when you are working on a crisis on your campus. My parents in Illinois and my grandmother in Brooklyn used the university's online updates to keep track of what was happening. They were able to leave messages for me. One family member became my personal point person: I would send updates to my sister, and she would contact the other members of my family.

I used the resources of the university (the crisis counselors who were working with us) to debrief, and my pastor and his wife were of great support. I had dinner with them several times during the crisis, and I met with my pastor to talk through the experience. He was able to help me see what I had contributed at a time when I was worn out and questioning my actions. We must have university procedures for dealing with crisis, but we must also pay attention to the human aspects, which make a world of difference. It is these human aspects that stand out in my memories of the campus tragedy. They help me understand that we can find good even in the midst of tragedy.

References

Boland Hall Fire. (2000). Retrieved July 29, 2005, from Seton Hall University, Department of Public Relations and Marketing Web site: http://admin.shu.edu?bolandhall/media/a11912pm.html.

Diamond, S. (2003). *Statement regarding indictment of individuals for alleged roles in Boland Hall fire.* Retrieved July 29, 2005, from Seton Hall University, Department of Public Relations and Marketing Web site: http://admin.shu.edu/bolandhall/diamond_statement.html.

Student Apartment Fire

Brent G. Paterson, Kristin S. Harper, Eugene L. Zdziarski, and Ann C. Goodman

In this description of the Critical Incident Response Team's response to the apartment fire, we have used first names for easier reading. We have also included comments from the authors that reflect their thoughts and feelings at the time of the incident.

Early on a Saturday morning, Ann, the Critical Incident Response Team (CIRT) on-call person, received a page from the College Station Fire Department that there was a fire in an apartment complex housing Texas A&M students. As she approached the apartment complex, Ann could see billowing black smoke and fire leaping through the roof. When she arrived, fire department personnel directed her to a vacant apartment in the complex in which approximately 20 residents had gathered.

> ***Ann:*** *It was 4:30 a.m. when the pager went off. I jumped out of bed as soon as I heard the shrill, beeping sound and went to the kitchen to call the university police. They told me that the College Station Fire Department was requesting assistance at a fire at the University Apartments. I pulled on my student life department shirt, jeans, and jacket and headed to the apartment complex, not knowing what to expect.*
>
> *When I arrived at the complex, I could see a large number of residents standing outside watching the firefighters. I went directly to the fire department command vehicle and identified myself. The command chief sent me to a vacant apartment that the manager had opened for the residents of the affected apartments, who were waiting for the Red Cross volunteers. Most of the residents were students; they were sitting on the floor, leaning against the walls, wearing bathrobes and slippers or flip-flops, or wrapped in blankets. Many were talking on cell phones. They all looked scared and shocked. I thought, "Where do I start?"*

After talking to some of the students, Ann called Brent and informed him of the developing situation. Brent headed to the apartment complex, but while he was enroute Ann learned from the apartment manager and fire chief that two students had been transported to a local hospital. Brent changed direction and drove to the hospital.

Ann remained at the scene of the fire and began to collect the names and student ID numbers of all the residents in the room. Several were not students at Texas A&M but attended the local community college or the university 40 miles outside of town. Ann told them that she would be available to assist them however possible, including contacting faculty members at their schools to verify the tragedy and making sure they got whatever university support they might need. She lent her cell phone to several students so they could call their parents to let them know about the fire and assure them of their well-being.

At the hospital, Brent learned that one student was being treated for serious burns and the hospital was attempting to contact his parents. Another four students who had been in the same apartment did not suffer any injuries and were in the emergency room waiting area. Brent then called the other two CIRT members. Kristin joined him at the hospital, while Gene served as communications coordinator. It was Gene's responsibility to gather information from the Student Information Management System (SIMS) on the injured student, the other students who had been in that apartment, other displaced students, and their families. Brent called the vice president for student affairs to apprise him of the situation; the vice president received updates throughout the day. Later, Gene called the director of media relations to discuss the situation. Brent: Since Ann seemed to have things under control at the apartment complex, I headed to the hospital to check on the status of the students. I didn't know what to expect. Fortunately, we had established an excellent working relationship with the ER staff. They apprised me of the situation and pointed out the students who were not seriously injured. I realized that I would need help.

This was the first incident that required the involvement of all four of us at the same time. We had discussed such an eventuality and used the communications coordinator in tabletop exercises, but putting these concepts into practice was different. Because Gene had access to the student database from home, it was natural to ask him to serve as communications coordinator. Kristin's empathy for the needs of parents was a good balance for my focus on making sure all the right people were contacted and the practical needs of the students were addressed.

> *Gene: I got a call from Brent about an hour after Ann received the initial page regarding the fire. Brent explained that Ann was at the apartment complex and he was at the hospital. Because of the number of students affected by the incident, he had asked Kristin to assist him at the hospital. He asked me to serve as the home base to which everyone could relay information and to look up student information on SIMS. Since one of my responsibilities as associate director of student life was supervising the department's information technology resources, I had home access to virtually all the departmental and university networks and databases. Although we had talked about using this type of coordinated deployment, this was the first time we had actually done it. I agreed with the logic behind our assignments, but it was difficult to stay at home while my colleagues were in the thick of things. I wanted to be actively engaged in helping people rather than simply plugged into a telephone in front of a computer screen.*

ER personnel informed Kristin that the severely burned student would be transported by life flight helicopter to the burn unit at a Houston hospital 100 miles away. They gave her the cell phone number of the student's parents. Kristin called the parents and remained in contact with them as they drove to the Houston hospital. She was able to give them updates on their son's condition and describe the arrival of the life flight helicopter at the College Station hospital and its departure for Houston.

> *Kristin: At the time of this incident, our hospital emergency room was quite small. In fact, from the visitor seating area, you could hear the medical personnel treating patients; sometimes hospital staff just leaned through the admitting window to talk to friends and family members of those being treated. As a member of the CIRT, I was allowed to enter the treatment area and speak directly to medical staff and the students being treated. And so it was that the doctor handed the phone to me to talk to the parents of the student most severely burned in the fire.*
>
> *Standing next to the student, I relayed his words to his parents and kept them informed of the treatment he was receiving. Eventually, I moved outside the treatment area to*

discuss more details with the parents, including whether they should drive the 100 miles to College Station. The hospital staff had asked me to dissuade them from making this trip, since their son was going to be transferred by air to a burn center at a Houston hospital. The issue was timing: Could they get to College Station in time to see him before he was transferred?

Although their son's injuries were not life-threatening, I never questioned the parents' need to act. When it was determined that the transport would likely take place before they could get to our hospital, I decided that it was my job to help them through the wait. For the next hour, in regular phone calls, I relayed to them their son's appearance, his level of consciousness, and the treatment he was receiving. I was on the phone with them when the helicopter landed on the hospital's rooftop landing pad. I described the helicopter's departure ("They're loading, the doors are closing, they're taking off...") and gave them specific instruction on where to meet their son at the receiving hospital.

I was thoroughly relieved when I reported the helicopter's departure. While I was on the phone with the student's parents, I empathized strongly with their urgent desire to get to the side of their injured child. I also felt a little awkward with the intimacy involved in relaying messages from their son and being their "eyes." On the other hand, I knew I was doing the right thing, for the student and his parents, and for the hospital staff. As always, that left me with a sense of pride and accomplishment.

As Kristin and Brent identified and worked with the students who lived in or were visiting the apartment where the fire originated, they discovered that one resident could not be accounted for. They relayed this information to Ann, who said that she had been hearing a similar story from students who had been in the apartment. Ann overheard several students talking about a third roommate and wondering where he was. Two students explained to Ann that the third roommate had gone out to get cigarettes at a convenience store down the street around 3:30 a.m. They never saw him return and figured that he had met up with some other friends who lived in the same apartment complex. We (Ann, Brent, and Kristin) realized that it was possible that the missing student was still in the apartment and had died in the fire. The students had not yet considered this possibility.

Kristin: After the severely burned student was transported to Houston, I focused my attention on the other students at the hospital. I stayed with them in the hospital cafeteria, answering questions and offering drinks and blankets. I listened to their conversation and their eventual realization that one of their roommates was missing. Each student shared what he or she knew of the roommate's location: Did he go out? Was he with friends in another unit? Did he usually sleep on the sofa? Did he die in the fire?

Brent: I was surprised that the residents of the apartment where the fire originated did not immediately notice their missing roommate. Perhaps they were in shock and were focused on the roommate who was burned. Later, in casual conversation among themselves, one person said, "You know, I haven't seen Paul." Another said, "The last I saw him he was in the bathtub. He liked to take long baths and sometimes fell asleep in the tub."

A few minutes after Ann overheard this conversation, the fire chief called her outside to tell her that they had found a body in the apartment where the fire originated. Ann told the fire chief what the students had said and the information Brent had shared with her about a missing roommate.

> **Ann:** *My heart sank, because I knew immediately that this was the third roommate. It was one of the worst feelings in the world— listening to these students speculate on the whereabouts of their roommate and knowing that he had died. They were obviously worried about him and had gone so far as to check to see if his car had been moved from the parking lot. Several were hopeful that because they couldn't find his car that meant that he had gone somewhere.*

Kristin and Brent decided to move the roommates and friends who had been in the apartment to a private area of the hospital. We wanted to avoid contact between these students and others arriving at the hospital. The students would need time to process what had happened. Another reason for moving them was to control speculation and rumors. We knew that they would eventually figure out that their missing roommate had died in the fire. We wanted to be certain that authorities notified the next of kin first.

> **Kristin:** *It was our practice to be sure family members of deceased and injured students were notified before discussing the incident with their roommates and friends. I knew the next of kin had not yet been notified, but it was very difficult to hear his roommates and friends speculate on his fate when I knew he had died. When it was clear to me that the students had come to that conclusion on their own, I found Brent and asked if we could tell the roommates about the death and ask them to respect the need to notify the family before sharing the information with others.*

Shortly after we moved them to a private area, the students began to verbalize their suspicions that their roommate and friend had died in the fire. At this point, we told the students that he had died and discussed with them the importance of not talking with others about the death until his family could be notified. We asked them to help us identify who was close to the deceased student and might need assistance from the university. We also discussed the grieving process and the students' immediate plans.

Meanwhile, Gene had been busy collecting information from the student database on the students affected by the fire; initially those who lived in the apartment where the fire originated and eventually all students who had been affected by the fire. Gene informed media relations of the incident and contacted residence life to see what spaces might be available to house students displaced by the fire. As he was gathering information on the student who died in the fire, he discovered that the student appeared to have a sibling at the university. Almost simultaneously, the students at the hospital were telling Kristin and Brent that their deceased roommate had a sister at Texas A&M.

> **Gene:** *Information was relayed to me from the scene and from the hospital that a student had died in the fire and emergency personnel were looking for contact information for the next of kin. I began a name search in the database to see if I could find information on the student.*

My wife, who had been awakened by the early morning phone call, came into the room to see what was going on. I explained that I was trying to find information on a student whom we had just learned had died in the fire. As a financial aid counselor at the university, Cheri is adept at using the student database. She looked over my shoulder as we scanned the results from the name search. I found the student's name and pressed the key to go to the next screen. Cheri said, "Go back." I went back to the previous screen. She said, "See those two names? They have the same permanent address." Then she let out a gasp: "They have the same birthday!" The shock of our discovery hit us. Tears filled Cheri's eyes. Not only did the deceased student have a sister at the university, but they were twins. We could only imagine how difficult it would be for his twin sister when she learned the news.

I relayed the contact information for the parents to Ann and the fire department. I told them about the twin sister and gave them her contact information as well. Although we wanted to follow up with the sister, protocol dictated that emergency personnel make contact with the parents. We also thought that the sister might take the news better if it came from her parents.

The fire chief told Ann that the blaze was under control. The fire had been confined to two apartments; however, the entire building suffered significant smoke and water damage. In all, nine apartments were uninhabitable. Ann and the Red Cross volunteer explained to the residents of those apartments that they should make arrangements to spend the rest of the morning with friends or family. Because the fire department or police had not officially identified the victim or notified the next of kin, we did not share the information about the death of the resident with these students.

__Ann:__ I went back outside to watch the firefighters clean up the scene and cordon off the area. Investigators were already on site to determine the origin of the fire. As the sun began to rise, I realized how cold and wet I was. The ground around the apartment complex was wet and muddy from recent rains and the water from the fire trucks. I wished that I had worn boots and a heavier jacket.

I felt completely helpless knowing that very soon these students, who were already in shock because of the loss of their apartments and belongings, would soon find out about the death of their friend. I called Brent to check in with him and let him know that the fire had been contained, then joined Brent and Kristin at the hospital. I wanted someone familiar to talk with who was probably feeling some of the same feelings I was experiencing.

By this point, the severely burned student had arrived at the hospital in Houston. Knowing that their other roommate and friend had perished in the fire, the students we had moved to the private area decided that there was no need for them to stay at the hospital. We collected information on how we could contact them over the next 48 hours and gave them our names and contact information.

The authorities were unable to contact the parents of the deceased student, so it was decided that his twin sister should be told. The fire marshal, a city police officer, Ann, and Brent drove to the sister's off-campus apartment. On the way, we discussed who would tell her. Everyone looked at Brent. He was the only one who had experience delivering such a message, so he agreed to do it.

Ann: Although my part in the overall response was essentially complete and Brent suggested that I go home to my family, I couldn't do that, knowing that work remained to be done. It was one of the most complex critical incidents I had ever been involved with, and I felt that I needed to see it through to the end. Thus, I decided to accompany Brent to the sister's apartment.

The roommate answered the door and was shocked to see a police officer, fire marshal, and two university officials. She woke the sister of the deceased, and we gathered in the living room. Brent told her what had happened and explained that we had been unable to contact her parents. We asked her to try to contact them while we were there. She was able to reach her parents and delivered the tragic news. The roommate said she would look after the sister, so we left the apartment.

Brent: Telling a parent, sibling, roommate, or significant other that a loved one has died is not something I imagined I would ever do; but I have been the bearer of such news more than once. I assumed that the fire marshal and the police officer had experience and training in delivering such a message, but they did not, so informing the student of her twin brother's death became my responsibility.

There is no easy way to share such terrible news. It is best to be short and direct. When the recipient is ready, more details can be shared. In this situation, it was critical that the sister's roommate be there to support her. I have asked myself how I am able to deliver these messages without losing self-control. Somehow, I am able to separate my responsibility in responding to a crisis from my own emotions. In our team meetings, we often discussed boundaries; it is easier for some than others to establish them.

We arranged to meet with the students who were affected by the fire. That afternoon, Brent and Ann joined the owner and management of the apartment complex, a representative from the local chapter of the American Red Cross, and the students at the apartment complex party room. Ann and Brent explained that the university would provide them with residence hall spaces. We would also notify their professors, help them replace destroyed or damaged textbooks and school supplies, and help in any other way we could. The apartment management made arrangements for students to move into vacant apartments. The American Red Cross offered vouchers for basic needs—clothing, toiletries, linens, and food. Before we left, we collected the students' names and contact information and told them how they could contact us.

Also that afternoon, Brent spoke with the mother of the deceased student and learned that the stepfather was returning from business in Seattle. He made arrangements to meet with the family when they came to College Station.

Brent: When I met with the family of the deceased student, they were looking to me for guidance. We discussed the mechanics of student records and financial aid and discussed counseling assistance for the sister. These conversations were more awkward than any similar ones I had experienced in the past, because they involved a mother, stepfather, sister, and two younger brothers. I was uncertain how to phrase my comments in front of the young boys and wondered what they were thinking.

It was clear from the conversation that the parents were struggling with a way to remember their son. The sister wrote poetry and had been working on a special poem since she learned of her brother's death. I suggested that we hold a campus memorial service for their son's friends and classmates. They liked this idea, but did not know where to begin. I asked if they would want to involve clergy. They said that they did want to involve clergy, although they were not very religious. I offered to contact one of the campus ministers on their behalf, not knowing whom I would contact or how he or she would react. I called the president of the campus ministry organization, explained the situation, and made an appointment for the family to visit with him later that day. Fortunately, he was agreeable to working with the family on a memorial service.

I have found that attending a memorial service for a deceased student is helpful for family, friends, roommates, classmates, and those of us who responded to the incident. It helps bring some closure.

On Monday, we contacted the professors of all the affected students and asked for their understanding regarding the students who lost many of their possessions in the fire and those who lost a roommate and friend. We worked with the campus bookstore to replace lost books and school supplies. In the subsequent days and weeks, we maintained regular contact with the affected students.

Brent: On Monday, I received a call from one of the students who had been affected by the fire. He said that he had an exam that day and that the professor would not excuse him and was giving him a zero for the test. I told him I would see what I could do. I called the associate dean of the college where this professor taught and explained the situation. The dean did not think the professor was being fair to the student but emphasized that the professor determines grading in each class. The associate dean offered to call the professor and talk to him; he called me back to report that the professor would not change his mind. I pleaded with the associate dean for compassion. He said that he felt very sorry for the student, but there was no way he could change this professor's mind. I was very frustrated as I reported the news to the student. I explained that there was a formal appeal process and that I would be happy to certify that he had been affected by the fire and could not reasonably have prepared for the test. With all that was happening in the student's life as he attempted to return to some sense of normalcy, he decided not to appeal; in the end, he dropped the class.

The Critical Incident Response Team worked very well in relation to this incident. We were very proud of the efforts each of us made in responding to the needs of the students and their families. We did not appreciate at the time the emotional toll responding to these incidents would take on each of us. We had a process for reviewing what had occurred, but we did not have one for emotional debriefing. Later we would discover and adopt the Critical Incident Stress Management process.

About the Editor-Authors

Kristin S. Harper is interim associate dean for undergraduate programs at Texas A&M University. Before this appointment, she was the senior associate director of student life, supervising alcohol and drug education programs, gender issues education services, student conflict resolution services, services for students with disabilities, new student programs, and adult, graduate, and off-campus student services. She also created programs for student families. She has directed the creation and implementation of learning outcomes for undergraduate student programs and services, and currently serves on the Division of Student Affairs Assessment Team. Kristin was among the first members of the student affairs staff to have on-call responsibilities with the Critical Incident Response Team (CIRT). She is a liaison with the Campus Ministry Association and, through this work, has developed and presented programs to ensure successful relationships between universities and campus ministries, especially in times of student and community crisis. Her previous positions include interim dean of student life at Texas A&M and dean of student life at Sul Ross State University in Alpine, Texas.

Kristin has a B.A. from Michigan State University and an M.S. from Texas A&M. She has 20 years of professional experience in college student affairs and three years of experience with the Boy Scouts of America. She has been recognized by Texas A&M as an Outstanding Professional Staff Member and is a recipient of the university's Women's Progress Award. As a member of the CIRT, she was recognized as a member of the Division of Student Affairs Outstanding Team in 1999. She is a Woman of Distinction with the Permian Basin Girl Scout Council.

Brent G. Paterson joined the administration at Illinois State University (ISU) in April 2001 as associate vice president for student affairs. He supervises the Career Center, disability concerns, student counseling services, and student health services. He is responsible for divisionwide strategic planning, assessment, and resource allocation. He also coordinates the Division of Student Affairs crisis response team. Previously, Brent was a member of the student affairs staff at Texas A&M for 17 years, serving in various roles. In his last position at Texas A&M, he was dean of student life and adjunct associate professor of educational administration.

As the newly appointed director of student life at Texas A&M in 1995, Brent was charged with developing a crisis response plan and crisis response team for the Division of Student Affairs. He guided the Critical Incident Response Team for six years in its response to hundreds of incidents. In 2001, he established a crisis response team at ISU. Brent has presented programs on crisis response at state and regional meetings.

Brent has a B.S. from Lambuth University, an M.S. from the University of Memphis, and a Ph.D. from the University of Denver. He has been active in the National Association of Student Personnel Administrators (NASPA), the Southern Association for College Student Affairs (SACSA), and the Association for Student Judicial Affairs (ASJA), holding leadership positions in all three associations. In 1999, he received the D. Parker Young Award from ASJA for outstanding scholarly and research contributions in the area of higher education law.

He was co-author of *Academic Integrity and Student Development: Legal Issues and Policy Perspectives*; editor and contributing author of *The Administration of Campus Discipline: Student, Organization and Community Issues*; and contributing author of *The Administration of Social Fraternal Organizations on American Campuses: A Pattern for the New Millennium*. His articles have been published in the *NASPA Journal* and the *College Student Affairs Journal*, and he has been a reviewer and associate editor of the latter.

Eugene L. Zdziarski II is dean of students at the University of Florida, providing overall direction to one of six departments in the Division of Student Affairs. His office has primary responsibility for providing programs and services in the areas of new student programs, disability resources, Greek life, judicial affairs, off-campus life, and student government. As dean of students, Gene leads the Division of Student Affairs Trauma Response Team. He is also an adjunct faculty member in the Department of Educational Leadership and Policy Development.

Previously, Gene was a staff member at Texas A&M for 15 years, serving in a variety of roles. As associate director of student life, he was responsible for coordinating the training and development of the Division of Student Affairs Critical Incident Response Team and was integrally involved in the response to the 1999 bonfire collapse.

He has a B.S. from Oklahoma State University, an M.S. from the University of Tennessee at Knoxville, and a Ph.D. from Texas A&M. Gene's dissertation on crisis management in higher education is titled *Institutional Preparedness to Respond to Campus Crises as Perceived by Student Affairs Administrators at NASPA Member Institutions*.

Gene is chair of the Task Force on Crisis Management and Violence Prevention for NASPA and regularly speaks at national and regional conferences on campus crisis management. He appeared on a national broadcast satellite video conference on campus crisis response and co-authored the training workbook for the videotape series Preparing for Crises On Campus produced by the University of Vermont. Gene has written several feature articles for NASPA *NetResults* and was a contributing author of The Administration of Campus Discipline: Student, Organization and Community Issues.

Additional Authors

Ann C. Goodman is associate director of student life at Texas A&M, where she has a primary role in the student conduct process and supervises the Student Conflict Resolution Services and Alcohol and Drug Education Program offices in the Department of Student Life. She is one of eight on-call contact members for the Critical Incident Response Team and serves as risk management coordinator for the Department of Student Life. Ann is a certified Critical Incident Stress Management (CISM) debriefing facilitator and a certified mediator and neutral in compliance with the provisions of the Texas Civil Practices and Remedies Code.

She has a B.S. and M.A. from New Mexico State University. She has been active in the Association for Student Judicial Affairs, including serving as the director of the Donald D. Gehring Judicial Affairs Training Institute. She has also been active in the Association of Fraternity Advisors and NASPA.

Lora L. Jasman is director of student health services at Oregon State University (OSU). She has overall responsibility for comprehensive college health services, with 76 staff members who serve more than 19,000 college students. Lora is a member of the Critical Incident Response Team and chairs the Infectious Diseases Response Team.

She has a B.S. in bacteriology from the University of Idaho and an M.D. from the University of Washington School of Medicine. She completed an internal medicine residency and chief residency at St. Joseph's Hospital and Medical Center in Phoenix. Before coming to OSU, she worked in private practice and served on international medical missions. She is board-certified in internal medicine.

Lora is a member of the American College of Physician Executives and a Fellow of the American College of Physicians. She has been active in the American College Health Association, presenting at national conferences, and has served in leadership roles in the Pacific Coast College Health Association.

Dennis and Cathie Klockentager have been married for 30 years and make their home in Lake Jackson, Texas. Dennis is a system engineer at the South Texas Project Nuclear Operating Company, and Cathie is a sales associate for Dillard's Corporation. Dennis has a B.S. from the University of Maryland University College.

They had two children, Amy and Mark. In September 1999, their younger child, Mark, committed suicide. At the time of his death he was a 21-year-old senior at Texas A&M, majoring in marketing.

Dennis and Cathie serve on the steering committee and are active participants in the Brazosport Chapter of Compassionate Friends. Compassionate Friends is a national nonprofit, nondenominational support organization whose mission is to assist families in the positive resolution of grief following the death of a child.

James E. Martin is vice president for student affairs at Pensacola Junior College (PJC) in Pensacola, Florida. Previously, he was vice president for student affairs at St. John's River Community College in Palatka; associate vice president for student success at Florida Community College in Jacksonville; vice president for student affairs, dean of student life and enrollment services, and adjunct professor in the School of Education at Georgia Southwestern State University in Americus; and vice president for student services and director of athletics at Chaminade University of Honolulu in Hawaii.

He has an M.Ed. from the University of Virginia and a Ph.D. in philosophy, educational administration, and leadership from Bowling Green State University. His professional affiliations include the College Board, the Southern Association for Colleges and Schools, and NASPA. He has made numerous presentations to state and national audiences regarding hurricane recovery at an academic institution.

Larry D. Roper has been vice provost for student affairs and professor of ethnic studies at Oregon State University since 1995. He has held numerous positions in student affairs, including director of housing, associate dean of students, coordinator of multicultural affairs, and vice president for student affairs/dean of students. Currently, he is the principal investigator and project director for a Kellogg Foundation grant for the Leadership for Institutional Change in Higher Education initiative.

Larry has a B.A. from Heidelberg College, an M.A. from Bowling Green State University, and a Ph.D. from the University of Maryland. He is involved in both professional and community service. He holds elected and appointed leadership positions in NASPA and the American College Personnel Association (ACPA), and is an ACPA Senior Scholar. He is a member of the board of directors of the National Association of State Universities and Land Grant Colleges and a commissioner with the Northwest Commission on Colleges and Universities. He also serves on the boards of directors of such groups as the Aesthetic Education Institute; Center for Youth Services; Montgomery Neighborhood Center in Rochester, New York; Community Outreach, Inc. of Corvallis, Oregon; and the Corvallis Chamber of Commerce. He is president of United Way of Benton County, Oregon.

Larry has contributed to several books on student affairs leadership, including *Student Affairs: A Handbook for the Profession* (4th ed.); *The Art and Practical Wisdom of Student Affairs Leadership*; and *Creating Campus Community: In Search of Ernest Boyer's Legacy*. He has written articles for the Journal of College Student Development and *NASPA Journal*.

Arthur Sandeen was vice president for student affairs at the University of Florida (UF) from 1973 until his retirement in 1999. Currently, he is a professor of educational leadership, policy, and foundations at the university, where he teaches graduate courses in student affairs administration and higher education. Before coming to UF, Art was associate director of residence hall programs at Michigan State University and associate dean of students and dean of students at Iowa State University. Throughout his career, Art has been involved in responding to student crises. As vice president for student affairs, he was actively involved in planning and executing the response to the Gainesville murders in 1990.

He has a Ph.D. from Michigan State University and completed postgraduate work at Harvard University. He was a board member for the American Council on Education and received a Fulbright grant for study in Germany. Art has served as president of NASPA, and he received NASPA's Fred Turner award for outstanding professional contributions in student affairs and the Scott Goodnight award for outstanding performance as a dean. In 2001, he was recognized by NASPA for career contributions to the literature.

He has been a major advisor for numerous master's and doctoral candidates, and has written four books: *The Chief Student Affairs Officer: Leader, Manager, Mediator, Educator*; *Improving Student Affairs Leadership: A Case Approach*; *Making a Difference: Profiles of Successful Student Affairs Leaders*; and *Enhancing Student Engagement on Campus*. He has also written more than 50 articles and book chapters.

Edward G. Whipple is vice president for student affairs at Bowling Green State University, adjunct associate professor in the Department of Higher Education and Student Affairs, and a member of the graduate faculty. Ed oversees a comprehensive student life program, including residence life and intercollegiate athletics. He also oversees the university's crisis response to student emergencies. At Bowling Green and other institutions where he has worked, Ed has developed and implemented crisis procedures and rewritten codes of student conduct.

He has a B.A. from Willamette University, an M.A. from Northwestern University, and a Ph.D. from Oregon State University. Ed is vice president of the NASPA Foundation and a member of the *NASPA Journal* editorial board. In 2001 and 2003, he was director of NASPA's Stevens Institute, and in 2002–2004 he was president of the Ohio Student Personnel Association. He has served as international president of Phi Delta Theta and is currently national president of the Order of Omega, the fraternity and sorority scholarship, leadership, and service honorary.

Ed is the author of journal articles and book chapters on various aspects of student life. He is the editor of the monograph *New Challenges for Greek Letter Organizations: Transforming Fraternities and Sororities into Learning Communities*. Recently, he wrote two chapters for the higher education graduate preparation text *Student Affairs Practice in Higher Education*.

Dawn L. Williams has been dean for community development at Seton Hall University since 1996. The areas under her direction include university community standards (judicial affairs), Greek life, University Center operations, the Student Activities Board, student government, human relations programming, leadership development, student clubs and organizations, new student orientation, the Women's Resource Center, and commuter student services. Dawn is a member of the management team for the vice president for student affairs; one of the team's responsibilities is staffing Student Affairs On Call. Before she came to Seton Hall, Dawn was dean of students at Marymount College; senior research associate, Teachers College, Columbia University; coordinator, pre-freshman programs, City College of New York; and residence hall coordinator at Arizona State University, the University of Delaware, and the University of Wisconsin-Stevens Point.

She has a B.A. in psychology from Illinois State University, an M.Ed. in counselor education from Penn State, and an Ed.D. in higher and adult education from Teachers College, Columbia University. Dawn has been active in NASPA and is currently a member of the *NASPA Journal* editorial board. She is a member of the board of trustees for the South Orange/Maplewood Coalition on Race and co-chairs the coalition's Interfaith Outreach Committee.

Dawn's work in the area of spirituality includes presentations at the Association of American Colleges and Universities Network for Academic Renewal Conference and the annual NASPA Spirituality Conference. Her article "Life Path, Spirituality and Community" was published in the Seton Hall University Center for Catholic Studies Summer Seminar monograph.

Cheri L. Zdziarski is a financial aid coordinator at the University of Florida with more than 20 years of professional experience in student affairs. Cheri has worked as a high school and college relations representative, assistant head resident, admissions counselor, senior financial aid counselor, and scholarship coordinator.

Cheri has a B.S. from Oklahoma State University and an M.S. from Texas A&M. She has been a presenter at both the university and state levels in the areas of college admissions and student financial aid. In 2000, Cheri received university recognition for her assistance to Texas A&M students seeking financial aid for study abroad. During her 14 years as a financial aid counselor and university mentor at Texas A&M, she was twice honored by students as a "namesake" for the Fish Camp orientation program. emotional debriefing. Later we would discover and adopt the Critical Incident Stress Management process.